Nobody Told Me My Legs Don't Work
Journey of a Down Dog

Travis C. Yates

Copyright © 2018 by Travis Yates

All rights reserved. No part of this publication may be reproduced, distributed, or transmitted in any form or by any means, including photocopying, recording, or other electronic or mechanical methods, without the prior written permission of the publisher, except in the case of brief quotations embodied in critical reviews and certain other noncommercial uses permitted by copyright law.

*For anyone who has ever loved an animal
and been blessed to have felt that love in return.*

Contents

Foreword 1
Chapter 1 It Could Be Anything 3
Chapter 2 The Waiting Game 7
Chapter 3 Hope for the Best, Prepare for the Worst 19
Chapter 4 Five…and Counting 25
Chapter 5 You Need to Come to Terms with This 31
Chapter 6 The Cat That Could Sleep Anywhere 37
Chapter 7 How Deep Is Your Love? 42
Chapter 8 The Power of Positivity 54
Chapter 9 The Miracle of Dr. Ava Frick 62
Chapter 10 Return of the Jedi 68
Chapter 11 Let There Be Poop 77
Chapter 12 Not Ready for Rehab 85
Chapter 13 Finding a Miracle 94
Chapter 14 The Moment We'd Been Waiting For 100
Chapter 15 What's Going on Here? 110
Chapter 16 Round One in the Books 115
Chapter 17 The Breakthrough 120
Chapter 18 "I Didn't Think She'd Ever Walk Again" 125
Chapter 19 Everything Old is New Again 132
Chapter 20 This Might Be the Best We Get 139
Chapter 21 A Walk in the Park 144
Chapter 22 You Take the Good, You Take the Bad 150
Chapter 23 The Pet Parade 154
Chapter 24 Some Tips 158
Chapter 25 The Rest of Our Lives 164
About the Author 167

Foreword

Two weeks ago, I had a young Great Dane dog brought to me for therapy following a spinal stroke. He could not navigate his rear at all. I relayed to his "Dad" the story of Keegan. Even though I have not seen her since 2009, her story has remained an inspiration to share with other worried fur-baby caretakers. A week later Travis contacted me, asking if I would write the foreword to Keegan's story. Almost ten years after Keegan's incident I have received the opportunity to relive those months, this time through Travis' eyes.

    Every day I get to meet new families, presenting me with a seemingly insurmountable obstacle. My job, as I see it, is to enlighten them, give options, and offer hope. The area of animal rehabilitation has grown immensely the past 10 years. But to the family of a dog who is in terrible pain or can't walk, it is an unknown territory. And their greatest fear is that there is no hope. Saying goodbye is the last thing expected or wanted.

    Animals shape our lives. They can be a pleasure and help get us through difficult times, give us laughter, and teach us patience, compassion, responsibility, and unconditional love. Travis has done a wonderful job of sharing how his family was impacted by those animals they opened their home and hearts to. Sometimes by their choice, other times they were the chosen ones. He closes with insights, learned during their journey, which can help anyone with a dog that has lost function of bowels and legs.

The path for rehabilitation is easier to find now, but you still have to get on it. May the step you take to rehabilitation become your animal's yellow brick road.

-Ava Frick, DVM, CVC, FAIS

"Animals are the bridge between us and the beauty of all that is natural. They show us what's missing in our lives, and how to love ourselves more completely and unconditionally. They connect us back to who we are, and to the purpose of why we're here." — Trisha McCagh

Chapter 1
It Could Be Anything

My wife's 32nd birthday began as just another average day, save for the excitement of being her birthday. It was bone-chilling cold outside on the last day of January, with a cold midwestern wind blowing in off the Mississippi River. When the alarm sounded at 6 a.m. we decided to skip our usual morning walk with our three dogs and stay in bed a bit longer. When we woke for work an hour later we set about the routine of taking care of the dogs. Renea fed them all in their separate quarters and left for work. About 20 minutes later, a canine stampede followed me down the stairs as I headed to the basement to let them outside. Our seven-year-old golden retriever/chow mix, Keegan, was the last down the stairs. I was watching her a bit closer because she had been moving around gingerly the last couple days, and I was thinking about a possible visit to the vet if it continued. After a quick breakfast, I let them all back inside and headed off to work at the local college, Quincy University, where I taught and handled public relations for the school.

Later in the day I came home for lunch to let the dogs out.

"Let's go outside!" I called from the bottom of the stairs. Jedi, our rambunctious black lab, and Canada, a German shepherd/chow mix, both came running down the stairs at top speed, Canada crashing into Jedi's rump as I stood blocking the basement doorway. I let the two out into the backyard to do their business and went back inside to call for Keegan. She likes to burrow her way into close quarters and crawl in between the coffee table and couch, and it sometimes takes her a minute to dig her way out. Often when we'd call them for whatever reason; a walk, dinner time or a regular bathroom break outside, she would crawl like a soldier slithering underneath barb wire fencing to get out from under the table.

Knowing this, I waited a moment and then called for her again but didn't hear the familiar scuffle of nails digging into the carpet. I went upstairs and found her sitting calmly next to a chair in our living room. She looked at me with a confused expression on her face, and I returned a similar look.

"Come on, Keegs!" I said at the top of the stairs, but she continued her stoic pose. I went into the room and knelt beside her to get a closer look at her. When she did finally budge, it was clear that she was heavily favoring her left rear leg. She hopped along on three legs as we went to the top of the stairs, where she plopped back down. I took a step back to gauge the situation and tried to stand her up again. No luck, she wavered on three legs and then sat back down.

I immediately called our veterinary's office and told them Keegan was having trouble standing on her back leg, and I was bringing her in. Next, I brought Jedi and Canada back inside and set about carrying Keegan down the stairs and into our Mitsubishi Montero. We bought an SUV specifically for this reason: hauling the dogs around. I softly talked to her the entire way, telling her it was going to be ok and that she needed to be ok for her mom's birthday. Yea, we're one of those couples that consider our animals our "babies." It happens, ok?

I called Renea on the way and told her I was taking Keegan in for an injured leg. At the time Renea worked as a school counselor at the local junior high school and typically got off work mid-afternoon. Renea confirmed she would stop by the vet to follow up as soon as her work allowed. Before I went inside to the vet's office I wanted Keegan to go to the bathroom, so I set her down in front of the entrance. At this point she couldn't stand on either one of her back legs. Panic slowly began to set in as the gravity of the situation became eminent. I scooped her back up into my arms, no easy task at 55 pounds, and rushed into the Animal Medical Clinics building. Our family vet, Dr. Robert Reich, quickly came out and led us to an exam room. I set Keegan down on the cold steel table and tried to ease her nerves by resting my forehead on hers and stroked her neck and back. Dr. Reich, an experienced vet who appeared to be in his early 50's, tried to sweet talk her as well.

"Good girl," I said to Keegan as Dr. Reich began his work. He wanted to draw blood, which is never fun, regardless of species. Keegan was more upset about the cold table than the needle poking into her skin. She was quite the model patient so far, allowing her vet to poke and prod while sitting calmly on the table, accepting my love. Dr. Reich tried to stand her up on all four legs, and I watched in horror as her hind quarters wobbled left and right before falling without support from the vet.

"This is not completely uncommon in dogs," he told me. "It could be anything from a tick bite to a ruptured disk in her spine." Keegan must have sensed the scary range of diagnoses and began to whine and fidget. "We'll do the blood work and take some x-rays," he continued. "We'll know more when those come back."

Unfortunately, the test for a rare tick bite had to be sent off to Oklahoma City and wouldn't be back until next Tuesday. Today was Thursday. Five days is a long time to wait for clarity when watching your dog slowly lose the ability to walk. The vet technicians wheeled in a stretcher and I tried to keep the mood light.

"Look at this; you've got your own private stretcher!" I said to Keegan, fighting back tears. I didn't want her to see I was upset, so I kept talking upbeat to her. "Mommy's going to be in to see you after work. You gotta get better for her birthday, okay?" Ok, I adore my animals but don't normally talk to them in this fashion. But the current situation was no ordinary situation, and I very much felt like a parent whose job it was to keep everyone calm. As I continued my baby talk, the vet techs hoisted Keegan off the exam table and onto the stretcher.

"I'm sorry, Travis. We'll call as soon as we know something," Dr. Reich said, attempting to console me as I was trying to do with Keegan, but with less baby talk. Thank goodness for that. I left the office and slowly drove back to work, replaying the entire lunch hour in my head. Just one hour earlier I was driving home for lunch, thinking about the evening plans with my wife on her birthday. Now, I was leaving behind a helpless family pet who was no doubt scared, confused, and alone.

At this point in our relationship, Renea and I did not have nor had any plans for children. We were ten years into our relationship and five years into our marriage and up to that point we both felt our calling was to rescue animals. As many pet owners with no children do, we referred to each other as the "mommy" and "daddy" of our pets. When you take animals in, it is important to remember they are reliant on you for everything in their lives: food, shelter, good health, and most important, love. Animals are amazing creatures in the fact that all they want from you is love. As our home and our bank accounts show, we've fully embraced being the parents to our four-legged children. It is a role we cherish, and the bonds we share with our animals are incredible. I had no idea, however, how much we would learn and how much more bonding could take place until Keegan's story unfolded.

Chapter 2
The Waiting Game

We celebrated Renea's birthday quietly that night, at home with our seven other animals and the season premiere of one of our favorite television shows, *Lost*. Dr. Reich wanted to keep Keegan overnight to get a better idea of what was happening with her. She had not regained the use of her back legs, and the x-rays did not reveal any structural damage in her spine. We weren't even sure what we were hoping for. Something was obviously wrong with her, but we didn't know what or which was even the preferred option. Dr. Reich believed the best-case scenario was a ruptured disk in her back, which could be manipulated or operated on. He also hadn't ruled out a rare tick bite that can cause paralysis in dogs.

What we did know for sure that night is that our family wasn't complete. Renea and I both decided it would be better to wait to hear what the vet's prognosis was than to conjure up our own conclusion in our heads and tried as best we could to put it in the back of our minds. In an attempt at a bit of normalcy and in one of the worst cases of bad timing in the history of all mankind, I gave Renea her birthday present.

I had a custom book made for her as a birthday gift from all the animals, with photos and captions chronicling our lives with them.

Each animal had their own set of pages with our favorite pictures, memories and quotes. That, of course, didn't help the already heavy mood that hung over the evening, and we sat and bawled while looking through the book, especially as we worked our way through Keegan's section. Most of them were tears of joy, but they were mixed with tears of pain knowing Keegan was alone in a dark veterinary office that night and not burrowed underneath us in her usual spot between the couch and coffee table.

I anxiously awaited a call from Dr. Reich the next morning with an update on Keegan's condition. We were hoping to hear that she had regained some, or maybe even all, of the use of her back legs. The phone finally rang, and the news was anything but what we were hoping for. She had now lost the ability to control her bladder, and they had to manually express her to make her go to the bathroom. "Expressing" a dog consists of squeezing around the stomach until the bladder is located and then putting pressure on it to empty it. Keegan also vomited quite a bit overnight. They told us it was most likely a reaction to the precautionary tick antibiotic she was taking. She was also dehydrated, so they started an IV drip and put her on a steroid to reduce any swelling she might experience in her spine. With the cause of Keegan's paralysis still unknown, Dr. Reich set about the process of elimination while taking all precautionary measures to ensure she didn't get worse.

I spent most of Friday online researching cases like Keegan's. Because we didn't have an official diagnosis, it was tough to try to pin down what might have happened. One recurring recommendation was that when dogs lose the use of their legs, a specialist should be seen sooner rather than later. Things such as MRI scans should be done to see what damage has occurred. Unfortunately, it was now Friday afternoon, and I knew that meant most places would be shut down over the weekend, and we would likely have to wait until Monday before seeing a specialist.

After work I met Renea at the vet's office, hoping and praying for any good news. We sat together in silence in an exam room waiting for Keegan to arrive. When she did, it was a truly heartbreaking scene. The vet technicians wheeled her in on a stretcher with IV drip still attached. She had two patches on her legs shaved for the IV needles, a cone around her neck to keep her from pulling the needles out and was fighting a bout of diarrhea. It was a terrible sight to see, and when I looked at Renea, it was painfully obvious she was having a tough time holding it together. The sight made my heart break even more. Turning my attention back to Keegan, it was noticeable that she was in a lot of discomfort. Not so much in pain, but so many other things out of her control: being away from home, the vomiting, and diarrhea, losing the use of her back legs, and being kept in a kennel for two days were adding up; you could see it in her eyes. Dr. Reich was gone by the time we got there, and we spoke with another vet who told us the update was there was no update; everything was pretty much the same. We spent a half hour with Keegan and left when the office closed at 5 p.m. They assured us that staff would be in throughout the entire weekend to care for Keegan, and we made an appointment to talk to Dr. Reich Saturday morning during their weekend office hours.

Saturday morning was hard. We made it through the second night without Keegs in the house, and it was very painful knowing she was right down the street yet there was nothing that we could do for her. We went to the veterinary clinic at 11 a.m., and they wheeled her in on her stretcher. We gently took her off the stretcher and set her down on the floor. Her leg with the IV needle was now wrapped in tape, so we asked if they could remove the cone from her neck. I wanted her to be as comfortable as possible and didn't expect her to chew off the tape. One small victory for her, I thought.

Dr. Reich came in and gave us an update on her condition, which again offered very limited change and nothing for the better. I immediately asked about a specialist, and he gave us all our options. The nearest animal neurologists were at the University of Illinois in Champaign, the University of Missouri in Springfield, and a clinic in St. Louis. Animal neurologists. I didn't even know that was a thing.

"I would recommend the clinic in St. Louis," Dr. Reich said.

"At this point, we'll go wherever we need to," I answered. "Whoever can get her in first."

We waited with bated breath as he tried to reach the clinic in St. Louis to see if someone was available over the weekend. While he called, Renea and I discussed the possible travel plans. Thankfully we both had personal days available and decided we'd both take one to make the trip together, wherever and whenever it would end up being. It was at this point that I understood we both knew the gravity of the situation and that were committed not only to Keegan but to helping each other through the tragic situation developing before us. We exhaled when Dr. Reich returned, hoping our weekday travel plans were all for naught and we could leave immediately.

"I'm sorry, none of the clinics are open this weekend," he told us. Our hearts sank. "I'll make calls to all three places Monday morning, and we'll get her in as soon as possible."

"You say the word," I told Dr. Reich, "and we'll be ready to load her up and take her wherever we need to at a moment's notice."

We spent a few more minutes with Keegan, resigned to the fact that no improvement would happen over the weekend. Our hope now shifted to getting her into a specialist on Monday and going from there.

Society's love affair with domesticated animals coincides with the industrial revolution. The first pet stores featured only birds and permeated the U.S. beginning in the 1840s. By the end of the 19th century, animals were fully commodified and pet stores dotted the landscape of most major American cities. At this point they had already begun to resemble the modern pet shop, stocking a broader selection of live animals and the necessary supplies and equipment that accompany pet ownership. By the 1920s even department stores included live animals and pet supplies for purchase[1]. As the first big ad age boomed, pets and their accessories became commercialized, just another part of the advertising milieu.

In the shadow of the growing counterculture movement in the 1960s that fought for civil rights, women's rights, and against the country's involvement in Vietnam, a modernized pet industry was born. National chains began popping up across the country, fine-tuning the live animal retail process. By the end of the decade, two major trade organizations had been created. The American Pet Product Manufacturer's Association (now called the American Pet Products Association) was founded in 1958 and the Pet Industry Distributors Association was founded a decade later in 1968. In 1987, during the decade known for its excess, PetSmart was the first of several big box chain stores to open. The "pet market" that once brought about laughter within the sales industry is today a $69 billion-dollar-a-year business[2].

Despite the growth, there is still a bit of the Wild West mentality when it comes to operating a pet store in the U.S. This is because

---

[1] Grier, Katherine C. (2006). Pets in America: A History. The University of North Carolina Press.
[2] Pet Business. (2018). A Short History of the Pet Industry. Retrieved from http://www.petbusiness.com/A-Short-History-of-the-Pet-Industry/

there are no Federal laws regulating the care of animals in pet stores[3]. These stores are governed only by state laws, so the rules and regulations are not uniform and vary from state to state. If they exist at all. Only 29 of the 50 states even have pet store laws on the books. And even then, they might be cursory and offer no regulations on the individual stores[4]. The welfare of the animals housed in pet stores across the country is sparsely regulated and monitored. In fact, less than half of all states mandate that food and water be provided to animals in these stores. Most states lack a requirement of veterinary care in the animals until they are sold, meaning a pet store owner is under no obligation to provide medical care for sick animals up until the time of purchase. In today's capitalistic society focused on bottom lines and cutting corners to lower costs and streamline operations, this is particularly concerning. This is not an assembly line cranking out products to line store shelves. These are living, breathing creatures that feel pain, sickness and have emotions. The lack of regulation in this arena is frightening.

While this is not an indictment on all pet stores, the evidence exists that some are not properly caring for their animals. There are plenty of documented cases of pet stores neglecting animals, selling sick animals in need of immediate veterinary care, and cruelly euthanizing animals. The Humane Society of the United States and PETA (People for the Ethical Treatment of Animals) are also concerned that many of the animals sold in pet stores come from puppy mills. Some of these mass-breeding facilities have abhorrent conditions and animals are denied care from their mothers,

---

[3] Animal Legal & Historical Center, Michigan State University. (2006). Retrieved from https://www.animallaw.info/article/brief-overview-retail-pet-stores
[4] The Humane Society of the United States. (n.d.). Pet Store Laws by State. Retrieved from http://www.humanesociety.org/assets/pdfs/pets/pet-store-laws-by-state-pdf.pdf

socialization, exercise and veterinary care[5].

We are seeing progress. In 2017 California passed legislation that will ban pet store sales of cats, dogs and rabbits unless the animals come from animal shelters or rescue groups. It is an effort to stop animal mills and promote the adoption of homeless pets while lowering the population of shelter animals[6]. It is the first statewide law of its kind in the U.S. The argument could easily be made that more states need to follow suit, as the American Society for the Prevention of Cruelty to Animals estimates that 1.5 million animals were euthanized in U.S. animal shelters in 2016.

It was at one of these pet stores, innocuously embedded in the corner of a mall, that Renea and I found Keegan, though that was never the plan. Regardless, the chance encounter with a dog in the pet store just a year into our relationship is what started this entire journey. It was December of 2000 and Renea and I were living in Springfield, Illinois. She was working on her master's degree at the University of Illinois Springfield, and I was working at a home mortgage company. Our big plan that holiday was to go to the Rose Bowl in Pasadena, California with some friends of ours who attended Purdue University. Purdue was playing the University of Washington in the Rose Bowl, and we thought it would make a great vacation.

We came across the pet store while doing some Christmas shopping on a chilly Sunday afternoon and didn't know each other well enough yet to realize that neither of us could walk out of a pet store empty handed. We were both pet lovers, and already owned a

---

[5] People for the Ethical Treatment of Animals. (n.d.). Pet Shops. Retrieved from https://www.peta.org/issues/companion-animal-issues/pet-trade/pet-shops/
[6] The Orange County Register. (2017). Gov. Brown Signs Pet Rescue Act, Mandating Shelter Dogs, Cats be Sold at Pet Shops in California. Retrieved from https://www.ocregister.com/2017/10/13/gov-brown-signs-pet-rescue-act-mandating-rescue-pets-at-retail-shops-in-california/

cat, Akili, named after former Cincinnati Bengals quarterback Akili Smith.

We found Akili through an ad in the newspaper advertising free kittens. We drove by to check out the litter and found a litter of all-gray kittens save for one little black female. The house of the kittens' owners was filthy, and if we could have, we would have taken all of them. We decided to take one as planned, and Akili stood out. They were clearly getting rid of the kittens too soon because Akili could barely walk, as we soon realized once we got her home. She spent the ride home cradled in Renea's arms but once we set her down, she was wobbling around and falling all over the place. In her first few weeks with us she ventured into the bathroom and even fell into the toilet…twice! She eventually found her legs and grew into a happy, healthy cat.

A very tiny Akili

Unbeknownst to us at the time, we would soon bring home a companion for Akili. We walked through the pet store and came across quite possibly the most adorable pair of puppies ever seen: two little brown balls of fur rolling around with each other in their cage. We were immediately drawn to them and asked if we could take them both into the "sitting room," where potential owners can visit with the animals in the store.

The two puppies were sisters, and one just kind of sat there quietly while the other was rambunctious and jumping all over the place, nibbling on both of us and wanting to play. She was definitely the friendlier of the two. We gave them back to the employees to return to their cage and decided to walk the mall and talk about it. Random stores passed by as we walked the length of the mall three times, weighing the pros and cons of getting a dog. The biggest immediate downside was no Rose Bowl trip. After buying a dog, getting her spayed, making sure she had all her shots, and buying toys, cage, etc., there would be no money left for a vacation. Not to mention, who is going to watch a new puppy for four days? Nobody we knew, that was for sure. The biggest pro was that she was so darned cute and loveable! Somewhere during the third lap of the mall, we decided that she was just too cute and was worth giving up a trip to the Rose Bowl.

This particular pet store didn't really prepare you for being a first-time dog owner. Renea and I both had dogs growing up, but Keegan would be the first for either of us as adults. The store just rang us up, took our money and suggested a vet on the outskirts of town. That was it. No crate, no puppy vitamins or toys, just a "here you go." I wish pet stores would be a little more sensitive to new pet owners as far as preparing them for what's ahead. Regardless, we walked out of the mall that day with a little ball of fur tucked away in Renea's jacket as we headed out into the chilly December afternoon.

It had been such a rash decision that we had no idea what to name her, and by Monday evening, we still didn't have a name. I was leaning toward Kwame (pronounced Quah-Mee), but Renea hated it. She had a few names of her own that I quickly rejected until finally on Tuesday she suggested, and I accepted, "Keegan." It would be years later before we agreed on if it would be spelled Keegan or Keagan, but at least two days into her new life, she finally had a name. We took our newly named pup to the suggested veterinary clinic that week for her shots and to get spayed.

Baby "Keegs"

Potty-training was a challenge, as she seemed unable or unwilling to control her bowels and was pooping everywhere in the house. When it persisted, we took her to a different vet and discovered she had intestinal parasites, something the first vet missed. After a couple of weeks on medication, the inside pooping stopped, and we finally had a fully functional puppy.

Keegan hated her kennel, but she wasn't old enough to be roaming the house all day long (especially with her unfortunate case of the runs), so we had to keep her in one while we were gone. We had to physically place her in the kennel, and even then, she fought to get out before we could get the door closed. It was quite a battle until we found a secret weapon. Keegan was obsessed with a pair of bright pink underwear that Renea owned. It seemed no matter where they were, she always found a way to find them and drag them around the house with her, and they somehow always ended up in her kennel. She wouldn't go in her kennel for a treat, but if we tossed the pair of pink underwear in there, she would run right into the kennel after them. It became our morning ritual. Keegan would sleep with us in the bedroom; we'd take her outside when she started whining in the morning, then with the aid of the pink underwear we would get her into the kennel and start our day. It was the first sign we had a unique dog on our hands.

One night we were lying in bed watching television with Keegan in the middle of us when out of the blue she started barking and howling with all her might. We couldn't figure out what she was barking at, but whatever it was it had her (and us) seriously spooked. I got out of bed and did a quick once-over on the house to see if anyone had broken in, which as expected, wasn't the case. Back to the bedroom I went, where Renea was trying to calm Keegan down. We let her jump off the bed, and she ran to the culprit – herself. We had a full-length mirror on the wall between two large closets and she apparently had never noticed it before. She ran up to it and continued barking at her own reflection. The poor thing caught a sight of herself in a mirror for the first time, thought it was another dog, and went berserk. We laughed hysterically at her overreaction while Keegan carried on at the mirror, then finally picked her up and calmed her down.

Calming Akili down was another matter. Now eight months old, she was getting used to being an "only child" and didn't think too highly of Keegan when we first brought her home. Akili was a Daddy's girl from the beginning, always plopping down on my lap or across my shoulders. Her favorite hobby was cuddling up next to me as I sat at my desk or kitchen table doing homework. When Keegan first came home with us, Akili spent the first few days on top of the refrigerator, not sure what was happening, but none too happy about it. When she finally did venture down to the floor, all five pounds of furry Keegan would come running over, backing Akili into a corner. Akili would hiss loudly and rap at Keegan's head with her paw. Keegan didn't care; she just wanted to play. Eventually, Akili accepted the new addition, and we spent lots of nights on the couch together as a happy young family of four.

Akili "helping" with homework

Chapter 3
Hope for the Best, Prepare for the Worst

I awoke to an early phone call Monday morning from Dr. Reich, who told me Keegan had a one o'clock appointment in St. Louis with the neurologist. We quickly got ready and headed to the vet to pick Keegan up for the big trip. I padded the back of the SUV with our biggest doggie bed and a comforter, wanting her to be a cozy as possible for the two-hour trek. We hadn't seen her since Saturday morning and could tell she was happy to see us when we picked her up from Dr. Reich's office. He said there was no change in her condition, but her mood seemed to be better. The staff loaded her up on her stretcher one last time and brought her out to the rear exit of the building. All the vet techs said goodbye to Keegan and asked us to keep them updated on her condition. Our veterinary clinic was one of the more expensive in town, but what you get is the personal care you don't always find at the inexpensive places. Dr. Reich's staff is one of the best. We've seen them interact with our animals and can tell they genuinely care for them. It's worth a little extra for that kind of attention, even when you have as many animals as we do. Of course, you don't always think this when settling the bill with them, but once your pocketbook shock subsides, you're usually glad you did. This case was no different. The bill for examining Keegan, doing all the tests and blood work, medicines, and keeping her from Thursday to Monday was close to $1,300. We had a sneaking suspicion that was only going to be the beginning.

With the help of the vet technicians we got Keegan situated in the back and began our trek for St. Louis. It was incredible how sweet Keegan had been through the entire process. She was paralyzed from the middle of her spine down, lost the use of her bladder and bowel, yanked from her home, poked and prodded by needles and instruments, sloughed around by the vet, the vet techs and now us, and through it all, she remained calm and loving. That was Keegan's nature. While playing with one of our braver cats, Keegan would let the cat put his head in her mouth and would never clamp down. She would get down on the floor and roll around with the cats, never hurting them, even accidentally.

I printed out some literature for Renea to look over on the trip down, and we discussed some of the things we would need to know to care for Keegan until we knew what the diagnosis was. At the time we didn't have a big box pet store like PetSmart in Quincy, so we figured it would be wise to stock up on important things in St. Louis. We also made a list of questions we wanted to ask the doctor. The drive to St. Louis was not an easy one; the fog on the highway was terrible. Visibility was poor, and our route on Missouri Highway 61 was wrought with tricky curves. *This is going to be a long trip*, I thought to myself, flipping on the fog lights.

Since Thursday, I hadn't taken the time to stop and look at the scope of the situation. We had our paralyzed dog in the back of the vehicle, and we were heading to St. Louis to see an animal neurologist, something I didn't even know existed until now. We had no idea what the cause of Keegan's paralysis was, or if it could be fixed. We didn't know if this would be the last car ride Keegan would ever take, or the first of many she would need to take to St. Louis or somewhere else for proper care. Frankly, I wasn't allowing myself to stop and think about it until I knew more, and I think Renea felt the same.

We got about halfway down and decided to stop for lunch. Renea and I had both been on a health kick since the first of the year, and I decided it was time to put that to a stop and treat ourselves, if only for the day. A Dairy Queen sat less than a half mile from the highway near Bowling Green, Missouri, and I made a quick turn for the exit. We made sure Keegan was secure in the back and went inside. A few minutes later, we were back on the road, armed with peanut butter cup Blizzards. Roughly two hours after we left the veterinary office in Quincy, we arrived at the specialist with full bellies and full of hope for Keegan.

They led us into an exam room where another cold steel table awaited Keegan. The nurse laid a piece of carpet on the table, so at least we weren't laying her on the cold surface. After repeating Keegan's symptoms and situation to the nurse, we waited for the doctor. The animal neurologist, Dr. Holt, appeared to be in his mid-50's and judging by the dates on the certificates hanging on the wall, that was a pretty accurate assessment. He was short on people skills, but I hoped long on medical competence. He went right to work on Keegan, testing her reflexes and squeezing her nails to test for deep pain response. I was helping hold her up, and as I lifted her with an arm under her belly, the pee began to flow.

"Oh, boy, we've got some peeing back here," I said, not sure how to react. The nurse came over and quickly wiped up the spill. Dr. Holt didn't miss a beat, continuing his exam as if nothing happened. Renea consoled Keegan; she wasn't used to just peeing whenever someone picked her up and squeezed on her bladder.

Dr. Holt didn't sound positive. Keegan wasn't responding well to the pain tests and didn't have feeling up through her spinal cord until near her shoulder blades. An MRI would be needed to see what the official cause was.

"What's the best-case scenario?" I asked.

"Well, the best-case scenario is if she suffered a stroke," he said, sugarcoating nothing. "She might be able to recover some ability with physical therapy."

"And if it's not a stroke?"

"The worst-case scenario was if there was some disk damage that can't be repaired," he continued. We let that sink in as he continued with what felt like a knockout blow. "I won't know without doing an MRI, but there is a possibility that some or all of her organs could begin to shut down without proper blood flow."

This was the first time the truly worst-case scenario had been presented to us. I felt the air get sucked out of the room as I looked down at Keegan.

"By all means, let's go ahead with the MRI and find out what's wrong," I finished.

I think I heard cash registers clinking away somewhere in the background of the clinic. We had expected an MRI would be necessary, but knowing the expense, had hoped we could avoid it. We couldn't.

You tell yourself you should be thankful when you find yourself able to afford emergencies like this. Renea and I were in quite a bit of debt. Our college loans had just kicked in, and we had been working for quite a while to pay off our credit card bills. Just as we finished paying off one large bill, Keegan's injury happened. Thankfully, we did have enough available credit to charge her medical expenses on a credit card, but it was a tough pill to swallow for both of us, as we thought we were finally getting on somewhat stable financial footing. So yes, we were fortunate to be able to give our dog the care she needed but weren't awash with gratitude at the moment. But seeing Keegan lying limp on a table…the decision was an easy one and we knew it had to be done. I gave the clinic our credit card and told them to charge whatever they needed. I now knew what it felt like to truly be thankful that we could do that. The reality is that it would take us a few years to pay these bills off, but what was the alternative? Having no idea what was wrong with Keegan or how to help her heal? That really wasn't an option for either of us, so we sucked it up and charged her bills on the card.

The MRI would take place that afternoon, and although Dr. Holt would get the results back soon after that, he wanted a doctor in Columbia, Missouri to review the results as well, and that wouldn't happen until the following morning. We would have to leave Keegan in St. Louis for the night while the test results were reviewed, and a diagnosis could be reached. We had just gotten her back from our doctor in Quincy that morning, and we already had to leave her again. The situation was hard on Renea and me, and I could only imagine how frightening it all had to be for Keegan. At least in Quincy she was with some familiar faces. Now we were leaving her all alone with strangers in a strange place. She had to be sedated for the MRI, and thankfully that would keep her groggy until morning. We said our tearful goodbyes and left the clinic.

On the drive back to Quincy, we discussed our options about the different outcomes we could be facing. Neither of us understood half the things the doctors were telling us, and they hadn't given us anything definitive to expect at this point. We knew she would need a comfortable orthopedic bed and would need to be kept away from the other animals when she finally did get home. We stopped at PetSmart on the way out of town and purchased a giant bed, diapers, waterless shampoo, and most importantly, lots of doggie treats. One thing that certainly still worked was her taste buds, and if she had to lie in one place for extended periods of time, we were determined to make it as enjoyable as possible.

We were both utterly exhausted by the time we walked into our home in Quincy. We still had seven other animals that were waiting for love and affection when we walked through the door. Jedi was rambunctious as always. I don't think he even realized Keegan was gone. It was no surprise to me, however, that Canada seemed to know something was amiss.

Chapter 4
Five…and Counting

As the domestic pet population rose in the late 1800s, so did concerns about animal welfare. Though several organizations for the prevention of cruelty to animals existed, they did not co-exist. There was no unified voice in the fight to protect animals. This changed as independent voices in the fight to protect animals began to join forces. In 1866 the American Society for the Prevention of Cruelty to Animals (ASPCA) was founded[7]. Twenty-Seven independent organizations from ten states joined in 1877 to form The American Humane Association[8]. The American Anti-Vivisection Society formed in 1883. These early groups fought against animal cruelty, slaughter, unfair use in entertainment, and scientific experiments. The American Humane Association is perhaps best known for the "No Animals Were Harmed" certification seen in Hollywood and other productions.

By the 1950s, local independent humane societies were scattered across the U.S. landscape, focusing primarily on the welfare and

---

[7] Wayne Pacell. (n.d.). History of the Humane Society of the United States. Retrieved from http://www.waynepacelle.org/history-of-the-hsus/
[8] The American Humane Association. (n.d.). History. Retrieved from https://www.americanhumane.org/about-us/history/

monitoring of cats and dogs. In 1954 several members of the American Humane Association left the organization to form the Humane Society of the United States. The focus of the new organization was federal legislation, so they based their headquarters in Washington, D.C. The organization worked with animal shelters across the country to create best practices for rescue, adoption, and spay and neuter programs. The Humane Society of the United States also helped create federal laws that regulate animals adopted from shelters for testing purposes, a law known as the Animal Welfare Act of 1966. They later influenced the passage of the Endangered Species Preservation Act and would create policies that helped reform rodeos, slaughterhouses, and seal hunts.

The 1970s would bring about greater cohesion among the local chapters and the national organization. In 1972 five regional offices were created. This structure existed until the early twenty-first century when the organization decided to hire a director for every state to work with local shelters, residents and help shape state policy. Today the Humane Society of the United States has expanded its reach to assist in animal rescue operations during natural disasters and coordinate with law enforcement in efforts to shut down puppy mills, dog fighting and animal hoarding. And of course, they continue to assist shelters across the country with training and evaluating facilities, producing shelter magazines, and acts as their voice on animal protection issues. It is at one of these shelters where we decided to once again expand our family.

In December of 2001, we left Springfield for Carbondale, Illinois, where Renea could begin work on her Ph.D., and I would finish my undergraduate degree. We both enrolled in Southern Illinois University and took a trip to the area a few months before the move to search for an apartment. The events were laughable. The landlords should have been embarrassed to show such dirty, disgusting and downright dangerous properties to us. For whatever reason, it seems that landlords think college students live in pure filth, at least at the universities where I've searched for apartments. We spent two days in Carbondale and weren't shown a single apartment we would even remotely consider living in. Stains all over the carpets, holes in the wall, water damage to the ceiling, terrible neighborhoods; you name it, and we saw it.

We returned to Springfield without a lease and not sure where we were going to live. I don't know how we got the idea, but we eventually considered the option of buying a house. Renea and I had been together for two and a half years, and I had just secretly paid off an engagement ring, that's how sure I was that we would eventually be married. It was Renea who had to take the leap of faith because we were relying on her credit to buy the house. While she spent her college years studying and working hard, I spent mine working, traveling and having a good time with friends. She was the picture of togetherness. Straight A's through college, a master's degree three years later, and now working on a Ph.D. I was another story. I didn't really settle down until I met Renea a few years earlier. We were a perfect match. I loosened her up a bit, and she taught me the ins and outs of being responsible. We met in the middle, and it had been working so far. Now, with no place to rent, we decided that buying a house was a logical choice and a good investment.

Finding the house was equally comical. Our realtor spent an afternoon showing us houses in our price range. Towards the end of the day we finally came across a beautiful home with a nice fenced yard and even a sun room. I looked at Renea, and her response was all I needed to be sure.

"This is the one. We'll take it!" I said, on the spot. "We want this house."

"You know, I'm not sure if this is the right house," our realtor responded. "It seems awfully nice for the list price." She double checked the paper work, and indeed, the house she meant to show us was across the street. The house we were currently in was thirty-thousand dollars above our price range. Needless to say, she did not win any Realtor of the Year awards that year.

We crossed the street to look at a not-quite-as-nice three-bedroom ranch. Three words describe the house: green shag carpet. All through the house, green shag. Overall, the house was terribly outdated, but otherwise in good shape and close to SIU's campus. We decided we could give the house a little TLC and it would be just fine. Our realtor asked if we wanted to finance through a person she had in the office. We should have known better than to trust her with our financial affairs after the wrong-house fiasco that just occurred but figured that if we could keep working through her it would probably be easier. It turns out she was working with some fly-by-night con man who ended up leaving town with our loan information and the info of half a dozen other customers. We ended up having to rent the house from the owners for the first few months before finally getting a loan through one of the local banks. Once again, we passed on recommending her as Southern Illinois Realtor of the Year.

With a new home, more space, and only Keegan and Akili to share it with, we decided to expand our family. A little older and wiser this time around, we decided to adopt a dog from the animal shelter. It wasn't a no-kill shelter, and we certainly wanted to save a life. I always wanted a big dog. Growing up I had a small cocker spaniel/Shih Tzu mix, Bud, who still lived with my dad, and Renea had a small wiener dog. Keegan had grown quite a bit in the past year, so we went in looking for a similar size dog.

We walked up and down the aisle a few times, stopping when a dog would catch our eye. Every dog is cute; it's difficult to find one that isn't. We were looking for that one dog that said to both of us, "I'm the one." We narrowed it down to two, but eventually my choice won out. She was a black and tan six-month old German shepherd/chow mix who was very loveable. In fact, she jumped right up to me and was ready to play when we took her out of her kennel. I knew then that this dog was the one. We filled out all the paper work and made the appointment to have her spayed.

A week later, we brought our new dog home. We named her Canada. I always admired the country of Canada and was dubbed an honorary Canadian by a college friend from the Great White North, so we decided to honor thy country by naming our new family member after her. She and Keegan got along famously. We had fenced in our backyard, and Keegan was more than happy to have a pal to run around with outside. They enjoyed the occasional game of tug of war with socks and rope toys. Canada was a sweetheart 99-percent of the time; it was that one-percent we had to watch out for: supper time. I don't know if it is because she was raised in the animal shelter or if it has to do with her breed, but she was extraordinarily territorial when it came to her food. If Akili or Keegan came anywhere near Canada at feeding time she would growl and snap at them. We tried to train her, but when it came to her food, she had a one-track mind. In fact, when she knows it is time to eat, she goes nuts, jumping around and even drooling. It's quite a sight, this tame dog undergoing a brief personality switch three times a day. We made adjustments and learned to feed her in a kennel, away from Keegan and Akili. We finally settled in our new home in Carbondale, now a family of five with the addition of Canada.

Canada: "Is it time to eat yet?"

Chapter 5
You Need to Come to Terms with This

The next 24 hours painfully dragged on for Renea and me as we awaited the results of the MRI. Dr. Holt called us that evening and told us he had viewed Keegan's MRI results, but still was not sure what the cause of her paralysis was. He wanted to wait and confer with the specialist in Columbia before making a diagnosis. I was a bit frustrated at this point. *Couldn't you read the results of your own MRI?* I thought. *Why are we paying you so much money?* I calmed myself by telling myself two heads are better than one, and if I didn't like the diagnosis I would just go looking for a second opinion. This way we had two doctors looking at and discussing Keegan's possible outcomes. That night we went to Blockbuster Video and rented a couple comedies to keep our minds off the situation. It was now Monday evening. We'd been on an emotional roller coaster since Thursday, most of which was spent without Keegan around. We were ready to hear the news and move on to the next chapter, one that hopefully included Keegan being at home. We watched *The Gameplan*, starring Dwayne "The Rock" Johnson, a cheesy movie about a cocky NFL quarterback who changes his life with the help of his long-lost daughter. The Disney drivel was just what we needed to get through the night. We went to sleep with heavy hearts but wishful thoughts for a good diagnosis in the morning.

We both went to work the next day but had trouble staying focused. Around ten Renea was tired of waiting and called down to St. Louis. She called me shortly after and shared the news: Keegan had a Fibrocartilaginous Embolism, or FCE, which basically amounted to a blockage in the spinal cord. The layman's term was a spinal stroke.

"The blockage is severe," Dr. Holt told Renea.

"When can we come get her?" she asked, fighting back the tears.

"You can come down and get her anytime, and we will discuss her options when you get here."

I cleared my schedule for the rest of the day and notified my boss that I was heading back down to St. Louis to pick Keegan up. My employer, Quincy University, had been tremendous through this entire process, especially my immediate supervisor. I had missed a day and a half so far and was distracted during the time I was working. Nobody said anything to me except to offer well wishes for Keegan. This did not entirely surprise me, as QU is a Franciscan Institution. Franciscans uphold a deep respect for all life, and the caring atmosphere was needed during such a tumultuous time in my life. Renea called my cell phone shortly after I left campus to inform me that she had cleared the rest of her day as well and would come down with me to pick her up.

We met at the house and let Canada and Jedi outside and readied the SUV for yet another round-trip to St. Louis. Once the dogs had taken care of their business outside, we let them back in and headed south on Missouri Highway 61. The roads were free of fog, but this time a light drizzle fell, and the temperature hovered around freezing. We certainly weren't getting any cooperation from Mother Nature on these trips to St. Louis. Thankfully the temperature never dipped below freezing, and the roads stayed ice free.

There wasn't a lot of talk during the trip. Dr. Holt had been very vague about Keegan's prognosis, saving the detailed information for when we met in person. We didn't know what to expect, whether she was going to live or die. He told Renea if the nerve endings to her vital organs were damaged, we could lose her, but as of right now that didn't appear to be the case. By the time we arrived at the doctor's office, I just wanted to see our dog.

Before we could see Keegan, Dr. Holt wanted to meet with us to go over the MRI results and prognosis. We were led into a tiny room, made smaller by a large amount of foreign medical equipment and computer monitors. And then, finally, there it was. Dr. Holt pulled up several images on a computer screen and pointed to where the damage had occurred. It was in the upper spine region between the C7 and T1 vertebrae. We had a lot of questions to which there really weren't answers, specifically how and why did this happen? He explained how it was a rare thing that occurs in dogs, where material from their cartilage enters the spinal cord, blocking the blood flow. I stared at the image on the computer screen and ached beyond what I could comprehend inside. Seeing exactly where the damage was and the injury it left behind made me hurt for Keegan. More than anything I wanted a magic wand to wave the damage away and restart the blood flow to the lower half of her body.

"How do we fix it?" I asked with an air of desperation.

"Not possible," Dr. Holt answered. "It's not reversible. You need to come to terms with that."

As Renea and I sat in the sterile, cramped office staring at a small white blotch on a computer screen, a feeling of complete helplessness and heartbreak washed over me. I heard Dr. Holt talking, but he sounded far away, and his words weren't registering in my brain. I continued staring at the white blotch on the monitor as phrases such as "no surgery will help" and "put her down" echoed throughout the tiny room, still resonating as if it were coming from some faraway place. Unfortunately, it was coming from an animal neurologist who had recently been charged with the task of finding out why our dog was no longer capable of moving the lower half of her body.

"Do you want to see her now?" he asked.

"Hmmm?" I responded from a faraway place, eyes glued to the screen as if I could will the blockage of her spinal cord away.

"I'm sorry, there's nothing more we can do," the doctor told me. "We'll take you to her now."

But we didn't see her next. First, we had to meet with their physical therapist and then schedule a follow-up visit with him in a month. After we were hit with the bad news, we had to listen to one of the nurses run some things by us, but we weren't necessarily *hearing* her. We sat in yet another little room, both silently mourning the fact that the neurologist just told us our dog would never walk again and may even be in life-threatening danger if things worsen.

The nurse mentioned a sling, and that snapped me back to reality. We had a big task at hand…caring for our now handicapped dog. I figured I could zone out and let it sink in on the way home, but for now, we still had some work to do. We asked for one of the slings to help her get around at home, and thankfully they had them there for sale, with all proceeds benefiting a golden retriever organization, of all things. While somewhat poetic, I found it incredibly distasteful that after spending thousands of dollars at their facility, they were selling us a $10 sling and preying on our frayed emotions to make a buck, regardless of the cause.

Finally, after all the instructions were given, the nurses took us back to see Keegan. She was resting comfortably in the last stall in a row of four empty kennels. Seeing her lying there, now knowing the full extent of her injury, I felt completely helpless. She propped herself up on her front legs when she saw us and started to drag her body to the door.

Renea crawled into the kennel and sat down beside her. Our nurse carried on, but we were giving all our attention to Keegs. We finally had to leave her and go back to the exam room to discuss physical therapy. I was about at my wit's end of emotion. My heart was breaking for her, and we kept visiting and then being taken away from her. Now that we knew there was nothing left that the specialist could do for her, we just wanted to take her home.

The clinic's physical therapist came in with a bounce in her step and a bright attitude. She talked to us about some of the dangers a "down dog" faces – down dog being the term for dogs with paralysis – and discussed canine therapy sessions. They finally brought Keegan back in, and our therapist demonstrated the exercises on her. They consisted of range of motion exercises in her back legs to keep her muscles and tendons loose, massages, and movements on an exercise ball. One thing I noted was that the exercises weren't rehabilitation geared toward recovery but rather meant to keep Keegan's muscles from atrophying. The reality of the situation set in even deeper. This was long haul stuff.

Sensing the somber mood of the room, the therapist was trying her best to remain upbeat through the entire process. She even told us our options for dog carts – a doggie wheelchair of sorts.

After that, we parted ways. It all seemed a bit hollow to me. There we were with sad looks on our faces and an injured dog, and it was like, "Ok, see you later, good luck with that paralyzed dog!" I know the folks in Dr. Holt's office were just doing their jobs, and they were all very sweet to Keegan, but I would have liked to have seen a little more compassion and empathy, as well as more advice on care. They didn't give much instruction on many of the issues I read about online, such as food, expressing her bladder and ways to stimulate her to make a bowel movement. Instead, we were told just to "press on her belly" to make her pee, don't change her food, and the poop will just come out on its own.

As it turns out, expressing a dog's bladder is much more complicated than just pressing on the belly. First, you have to find the bladder, which is no easy task, and then make sure you express it completely. Urine left in the bladder can quickly turn into a bladder infection. A change in diet is also beneficial, as the average dog food we were currently feeding our dogs contained a lot of "filler." We did our own research and discovered that with a slightly more expensive food, she will get more nutrients and poop less. So far, her pooping habits had remained the same; when it was time, it just came right out. But sometimes that's not the case, and there are several different methods to coerce that sphincter to go into action. We weren't shown any of these methods but rather learned on our own after the fact. So, I suppose we were right to have left the clinic a bit upset and not fully happy with the treatment and care we received.

As Renea gathered Keegan's things, I went to the front desk to settle the finances. After leaving an $800 deposit the day before, we now had a $1,600 bill to pay. Total doctor bills paid in Quincy and St. Louis just so they could tell us she won't ever walk again? $3,600. That was just for the diagnosis. Pets aren't cheap, and with so many of them at home, pet insurance wasn't an option. Keegan was quickly becoming our own million-dollar baby.

Leaving the office, I hoisted Keegan into my arms, carried her to our car, and off we went. Even though the news was bad, and we weren't any better off than the day before (just a little lighter in the pocketbook), Renea and I were both relieved that Keegan was finally coming home.

Chapter 6
The Cat That Could Sleep Anywhere

On the way home, we decided how we would attack the problem. The first and biggest obstacle was deciding where we were going to keep her. Our house was a bi-level home, and all the animals remained upstairs except when taking them outside. Our back door opened to our fenced in back yard, and we decided that it would be easiest to keep Keegan downstairs, where she would be away from the other animals and close to the back yard. We didn't want to keep her downstairs by herself, but there were many factors involved in the decision. The first was the fact that she was a 55-pound dog and hauling her up and down the stairs just wasn't feasible for either of us. Second, we had no idea what her, umm, "potty" situation was going to be like, all we knew was she couldn't control where and when she had to go. Because of this, we would likely be taking her outside a lot. Having her near the door would help greatly. Lastly, she needed to stay on her orthopedic bed as much as possible to avoid rug burns and bed sores. Upstairs with the other dogs and cats, Keegan would be dragging herself all over the place and not staying where she should be. It would be best for everyone including her if we made her a special area downstairs where we could shower her with love and treats without the others getting jealous and in our way. We picked out a spot next to the brick hearth that housed our fireplace. It was a central location of the room, so she wouldn't be tucked away and would feel a part of things when we were watching television or on the computer downstairs.

Things were going well in Carbondale for both Renea and me. Canada was an excellent addition to the family, and we had started updating our 1970s style home to a more modern look, including new carpet and paint. Renea was moving smoothly through the doctoral program at SIU and was even asked to be a teaching assistant by the dean of the School of Education. She was also working as an adolescent counselor for a local state agency. I was turning heads at school, but the film program at the time was dismal, and I began to re-think my major. The University had a great Radio-Television program with state of the art equipment, versus the outdated and ill-equipped film program. It was late fall of 2002, and I hated the idea of starting over in a new program, but thankfully my credits from the film program fulfilled my minor qualifications. After two semesters, I finally made the switch from film to radio-television and switched my career focus to a career in television. I had several years of experience in television already and looked forward to returning to the industry.

Something else happened that fall that would change our lives forever. In mid-November, on a cold and rainy evening coming home from seeing a client in the neighboring town of Murphysboro, something on the side of the highway caught Renea's eye. She was curious enough to turn around and go back to investigate, and what she found was a small, malnourished white kitten soaked to the bone and covered in dirt. He came right up to Renea and gave a sickly meow. She picked him up into her arms and jumped back in the car.

When she was almost home, she called and said she needed me to come out to see something. I had no idea what she was up to but was not shocked when I saw she had a kitten wrapped up in a towel in her arms.

We brought the kitten inside and took him to a spare bedroom, away from Keegan, Canada, and Akili. He looked a bit like Yoda with big ears sticking up from his tiny head. We got him cleaned up and spent the rest of the night in the bedroom with him giving him lots of love and affection. He was quick to reciprocate. The next day we made an appointment with our vet to check the little guy out. He was in decent shape, our vet informed us on the day of the visit. He had ear mites and an intestinal parasite that would need medication, but other than that he was going to be okay. One last thing she mentioned before we left…he was deaf.

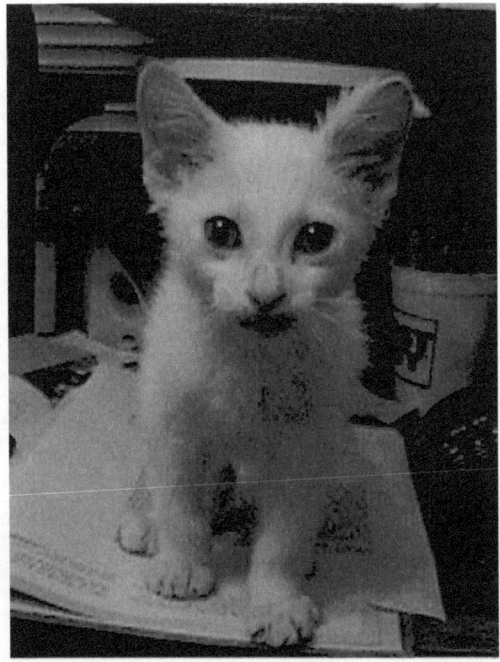

Our little Yoda

We named our new little deaf kitten Cha, after a song by our favorite band Local H, "Cha! Said the Kitty." Cha seemed to take on qualities of the people and animals around him, which means he ended up half human, half dog, and no cat. He and Keegan would roll around the floor, and Cha would let Keegan slobber all over him as he stuck his head in her open jaws. He loved to find unique places to sleep and being deaf made him a very sound sleeper. We would come home and find him sleeping in the most peculiar places: In a kitchen cabinet, buried in wires behind our VCR, in a gym bag…it seemed every time he was tired he went looking for a new inventive place to sleep. Finding him was a task, because he couldn't hear us calling for him. Sometimes it would be an hour before we'd finally come across him sleeping in the bathtub, in a closet or under a blanket.

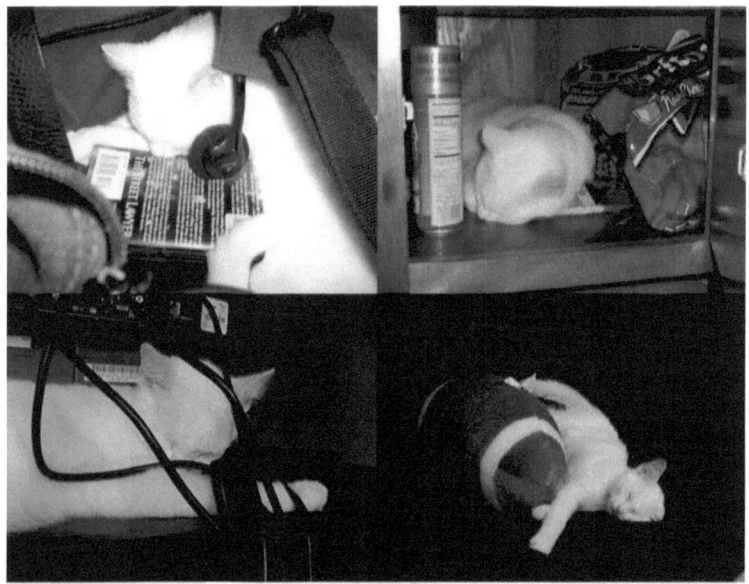

The cat that could sleep anywhere

Our family was quickly growing, and it wasn't about to stop. On a recent trip home to Quincy, I visited my father and found him unable to care for our dog Bud, who was still going strong at 12 years of age. Renea and I briefly discussed it and decided that we would be able to provide a much better home for Bud and relieve my father of the duties associated with taking care of an animal. We headed back to Carbondale with my old friend and familiar faithful companion in tow. Bud would go on to occupy the basement of our future home in Quincy a lot of the time, for the ease of not having to go up and down stairs in his later years and disagreements with the other dogs, which is why I considered it Bud's basement until Keegan's situation called for the passing of the torch, so to speak.

Bud was a funny old dog. He barely barked the first half of his life, but once we got him around Keegan and Canada, he acted as if he was saving it all up for here and now. Both Keegan and Canada would bark at a large picture window in our living room as people would walk by. Bud would be sleeping on the couch when the chorus of barking began. Without even knowing what he was barking at, he would sit up and quickly join in.

"Bud, you don't even know what you're barking at!" I would constantly say to him. He wouldn't even be looking in the right direction. Keegs and Canada would be barking at a dog walker outside and Bud would be looking down the hallway, barking with purpose at absolutely nothing.

He was a loyal dog, that's for sure. Everywhere I went, he wanted to be. If I walked into a room he couldn't go in, he laid down outside the door, waiting for me to return. He would sleep on the floor next to my side of the bed. He and I had been together since I was a freshman in high school. He'd seen a lot of my joys and heartache, and we shared a special bond. He didn't seem at all bothered by the host of new characters in my life, he was just happy we were together again, as was I.

With the addition of Cha and Bud, we were now at five...and counting.

Chapter 7
How Deep Is Your Love?

We finally arrived home from St. Louis with Keegan around 8 p.m. Tuesday night. It had been five days since Keegan's stroke, and she hadn't been home since. Renea and I were both exhausted but happy to have her home. The dogs had been inside since eleven o'clock that morning, so she ran inside to let them out while I unloaded the bevy of PetSmart bags with Keegan's things from the SUV. Once the dogs were back inside, I loaded Keegan up in my arms and took her inside to her new home in the basement. We put her new gigantic orthopedic bed down in front of the hearth and laid her down on it. As she got adjusted, we unloaded the treats, diapers, shampoos, and puppy pads onto our air hockey table in the basement. The hockey table was being transformed into Keegan's new supply station, our basement from a fun social gathering place to a medical facility.

Shortly after we made it inside, we got our first introduction into our new life.

"Oh crap, I think she's peeing!" Renea yelled. There was a comforter on the bed, so thankfully the new bed didn't get ruined. We ran over as Keegan looked up at us with a look that said *I'm sorry, it's not my fault*. It broke both our hearts.

"It's not your fault," I said to her as I hoisted her up with the sling around her belly. When I lifted her up, even more pee came out. "Oh god, there's more!" I yelled, quickly trying to get her outside.

Once we made it out to the patio, I pushed around on her belly to locate the bladder but couldn't find it. I called for Renea's help. She was already busy inside trying to clean up the pee on the blankets, carpet and tile. There was now a urine trail from the bed to the door.

"I'm cleaning up in here!" she snapped.

"I can't do this by myself!" I shot back. We had been home five minutes and were already at each other's throats. It was going to be a long night.

We finally got her to pee a little bit outside, and took her back to her bed, with a second comforter replacing the pee-drenched first one. After that long process, we both had to take a step back and breathe deep. Renea decided to go to the store to pick up some cleaning supplies, which we would obviously need, and a blow-up exercise ball required for Keegan's rehab. I went upstairs and paced the living room for a few minutes, then sat down on the couch to collect my thoughts. My head was spinning. My dog couldn't walk, or even pee by herself. We still didn't know about the pooping situation or what that would entail. Renea and I were a good team, but we were both high-stress people. In putting both of us in a volatile situation like this, I honestly didn't know what we'd gotten ourselves into.

After a few tears and a few deep breaths, I headed downstairs and told myself, however hard I think this is…it's even harder for Keegan. She lost the use of her back legs and the ability to control her own bowel movements. We just had to clean up after her and put her through rehab exercises.

My grandmother was an amazing lady, and she had a unique way of handling adversity. "I went into the other room, had my cry, and then got back to living," she would say about some of the more challenging moments of her life. She would allow herself a moment to be overwhelmed before putting a strong face back on, and my grandmother was one strong woman. Given our current circumstances, I questioned if I was a strong man. I had to adopt my grandmother's philosophy, I told myself, or I would never make it through this. So that's what I did; I had my cry, and headed downstairs to "get back to living," which in this case meant making sure Keegan had everything she needed, from a dry bed to proper rehab.

I opened the basement door and found Keegan sitting by the door. She had crawled from her bed a good fifteen feet to the door. The first of many times she would amaze me.

"Sweetie, you need to stay in your bed," I said, picking her up and placing her back on her plush bedding. I grabbed a treat to keep her busy and began straightening up the basement, which Keegan had already made a chaotic mess.

Renea came home from the store and I could tell she had cried most of the way there and back. Later, when she lay next to Keegan in the bed to calm her down before bed time, she started crying again. I wasn't sure what to say, except to tell her that somehow, we'd figure it out.

We finally got Keegan settled in for the night with a treat-filled KONG toy, dimmed the lights and headed up to bed. By the time our heads hit the pillows, we were both half asleep, more exhausted than we'd ever been in our entire lives.

A few years into our relationship, Renea began asking if I was ever going to propose to her. My answer was always, "relax" or "soon." My parents divorced when I was five, and although I had no doubts about our love, I made a promise to myself long ago that I would wait to be sure the woman I married was the woman I would stay with forever. Heading into our third year, we had a solid relationship, but nowhere near perfect (if there is such a thing). We were both still growing as people and learning about each other and our relationship. There were plenty of fights, some legitimate and some leaning towards the ridiculous.

I had known for a long time that I wanted to marry her. Renea had the idea to go engagement ring shopping one day while living in Springfield, perhaps with the idea of moving things along a bit quicker. She pointed out a ring she liked, and before we left Springfield for Carbondale, I owned the ring. I kept it hidden in a drawer for nearly two years before it finally saw the light of day. As the summer of 2002 approached, after three years of listening to Renea, our friends, and parents all asking me, "when are you going to get married?" my heart and mind told my soul to ask for her hand in marriage.

I picked our three-year anniversary as the day I would ask. I didn't want to propose in the traditional fashion, though. Because I made her wait this long, she deserved something special. I did what I knew best and started editing a video proposal. For a month, I spent some time each night in the computer room putting it together, using video footage and photos from our three years together. It was set to the song "At this Moment" by Billy Vera and the Beaters, most famous for being the breakup song for Alex P. Keaton and his girlfriend Ellen on the 1980s sitcom *Family Ties*. While we never had an official "song," Renea and I always agreed it was a touching scene in the series and a good love song. At the end of the video, a title card read: *There is no need to relax anymore because soon is finally here….will you…marry me?*

I rented a lakeside hotel room at the Rend Lake Resort in Southern Illinois for the setting. I packed us both an overnight bag, reserved our dog sitter, and loaded up the car. That afternoon I made the 45-minute trip north to Rend Lake to prepare the room. I set up a VCR so we could watch the video, hid the overnight bags, put a bottle of champagne on ice, put the tape and card in a gift bag, and lit two rows of candles leading from the entryway to the champagne and gift bag in front of the television. I was anxious enough as it was to finally propose, and little did I know some comical moments still stood in my way. On the trip back to Carbondale to pick up Renea, a car swerved over from the right lane into mine while on the interstate. I veered off the road and into the grass ditch between highways. Thankfully I was able to keep the vehicle on all four wheels and managed to get back on the road without causing an accident. That was strike number one.

When I finally made it home, there was a motorcycle sitting in our driveway. *What's this?* I thought. We didn't have any friends that owned a motorcycle. I had lit candles and champagne on ice back at the hotel, an engagement ring burning a hole in my pocket, nearly died on the interstate, and now some mystery biker at my house. I went inside and found a friend of Renea's family inside. I greeted him with a pleasant yet somewhat contorted smile.

"I'm just passing through on a road trip down south," he said. "Wanted to stop by and say hi." The thing about this friend, he's a talker.

So he talked...and talked...and talked. I did my best to keep my cool, but probably came off as rude and belligerent. Strike number two! I was wondering if some higher power didn't want this happening. Renea only thought we were going to dinner that night, and I didn't want her to suspect anything different by pulling him aside and asking him to leave. So I waited, projecting patience as best I could.

After about 45 minutes he finally left. I told Renea I was hungry and wanted to leave right away for our anniversary dinner. It's nothing fancy, I promised, before we left. Our favorite eatery at the time, Bob Evans, was on the way to Rend Lake, and until we passed it Renea assumed that's where we were going. *Gee, what a romantic anniversary* she had to be thinking at that point. *Dinner at Bob Evans, way to sweep a girl off her feet.* Confusion finally set in when we passed the restaurant and got on the interstate. I refused to divulge any information except that we were going to dinner. There was a restaurant at the resort that I planned on taking us to later for dinner, so technically I wasn't lying.

We finally arrived at the resort, and thankfully it wasn't on fire. My heart was racing at this point. I don't think I'd been so nervous around her since the night we met. We walked up to the room and I opened the door. Some of the candles in my romantic candle trail had burned out, but there were enough to still make it romantic. I led her to the bed, where she opened her anniversary card, and opened the tape. We popped it in the VCR and I sat back while she watched it teary eyed. The tears were a good sign…so far so good! I pulled the ring out as the video proposal neared the end, and once finished, she turned to me as I knelt on one knee. I'd had a crush on this girl since we had class together in the first grade. On the last day of the 1981-82 school year I wrapped a geode in notebook paper and left it on her desk. She never got it. I worked that little relationship fun fact into my proposal.

"I tried to give you a rock in first grade, but you never got it," I said to her. "I'll try to do it right this time. Will you be my wife?" At least that's how good it sounded in my mind. I was a crying, blubbering mess, so it was more of those words combined with sniffles and snorts. I barely got the question out. She was somehow able to comprehend me, wrapped her arms around me and said yes.

The first thing we did was run over and blow the rest of the candles out. They were tea candles and I didn't place anything under them, so the wax was running all over the carpet. It's a wonder I didn't burn the whole place down before we got there. I suppose I narrowly avoided strike three.

Once the shock wore off, Renea realized the ring was the ring she picked out in Springfield. I think that made up for making her wait so long. We opened the champagne and sat on the balcony overlooking Rend Lake, calling family and friends to tell them the good news. After dinner, we returned to the hotel room for more champagne and sat on the balcony reflecting on our last three years together and dreamed about what the future would hold for us.

Neither one of us wanted to wait a long time to get married, so we picked May 31, 2003 as the wedding day, in Quincy's Moorman Park. We probably would have done it sooner, but we both wanted the wedding to be outdoors, and the end of May was the first convenient date.

When May 31 finally rolled around, I was a mess. I wanted everything to be perfect, so I went out to the wedding site that morning. Several decorative props weren't delivered, the sky looked like storms were on the way, and some people were flying a kite next to the wedding set up. Well, the skies cleared, the rest of the props showed up, and a member of our wedding party kicked the darn kite fliers out. It was time to get married!

Our ceremony was short and sweet, for our sake, and more importantly for the benefit of those in attendance. We've both sat through enough lengthy weddings to know that short and sweet is often better. The wedding went off without a hitch, and in a few short minutes, I was kissing my new bride.

I was in love since first grade

We were now married with a sweet animal family of five: Keegan, Canada and Bud on the canine side; Akili and Cha on the feline side. Apparently, that balance didn't work because a third feline would soon be introduced to our already crowded house. In the summer of 2003 I landed a job as an associate producer at WSIL-TV, an ABC affiliate in Carterville, just 20 minutes east of Carbondale. It was the perfect setup for a senior in the Radio-Television program at SIU. I had an advantage with my previous videographer experience at WGEM, an NBC affiliate in Quincy. Plus, I was older than your typical college student by a few years, and that helped me advance quickly at the station. It was there that I met Sandy Mann, our human resources director.

"Travis, come with me, I want to show you something I found," Sandy said to me one day while passing through the newsroom.

I went into her office and saw an adorable gray kitten purring away on the chair. Sandy shared my love of animals and knew Renea and I had several at home, which is why she came to me first when she found a stray kitten under her porch. I went up to the kitten and she nudged her head against my face. She was obviously a very loveable soul. Sandy explained that they heard crying coming from underneath their porch, where they found the cat. No mama or siblings around, just the scrawny little kitten. Her husband was allergic to cats, so she couldn't keep her.

"I tell you what," I told Sandy. "I'll talk it over with Renea; you keep looking for a home for the kitten. If nobody takes her, I'll see if we can't arrange to bring her home with us."

I talked it over with Renea, and we agreed that if the cat were to go homeless, we would take her in. I don't know how hard Sandy looked for someone to take her, but the next day the kitten was still in her office.

"Alright," I told Sandy. "I'll take her home with me on my dinner break. She can join our family." After the six o'clock news, I cradled the little girl in my arms and made the 20-minute drive back to Carbondale to introduce her to her new home.

I was met with unadulterated anger as I walked through the door. Cha was not happy about this strange new being in my arms, and he showed me by hissing, batting and biting at my legs. Remember, Cha was primarily raised by the dogs and us (Akili pretty much kept to herself these days), and by proxy thought he was half dog, half human, and ruler of the castle. He had no fear and was telling me he wasn't happy with this recent decision. Renea and I took the kitten into the guest bedroom, much like the way we quarantined Cha the night we found him. We checked her over for ticks and mites, to which she miraculously seemed free of, and set about naming her. We thought we would keep the Local H trend going after Cha. The band's lead singer was Scott Lucas. They had just released a new album, "Whatever Happened to P.J. Soles?" and the drummer's name was Brian St. Clair, so we combined all three elements for P.J. St. Lucas, or simply PJ for short. This entire discussion was held with

Cha outside the door hissing and growling at a cat he could smell but could not see (or hear, even if he wanted to).

Akili really didn't care. By now she was used to the constant flow of new additions to the household. The dogs didn't mind either. Bud was probably the most curious. He would go chasing after PJ, scaring her half to death. If he did manage to corner her, all he would do is sniff around her until she was perturbed enough to bat at his nose. The entire process would end with him yelping and running away from a kitten. Bud would never be mistaken for the alpha of the house, that's for sure. It didn't take long for Cha to adjust to PJ, and the two surprisingly ended up best buddies. PJ loved being around Cha, and we would find the two cats lying together all the time, often with paws intertwined. I had never seen such a close relationship between two cats. Sometimes PJ would literally go searching for Cha, and then plop down on top of him once she found him.

Cha & PJ: best of friends

The next year would be a superb year for both of us. My new job was going well; I was quickly promoted to Head Associate Producer. Graduation was less than a year away. Renea had begun teaching at John A. Logan College, a local community college. We met an amazing group of friends at the TV station that consisted of four other couples. The year was filled with hard work, good times with friends, and a household of love with all our animals. To quote Frank Sinatra, it was a very good year.

In May of 2004 one of our producers left WSIL for a job in New York, which left a job opening. I hadn't even considered producing as a career option. My field was video production, but my news director came to me and personally asked me to apply for the job. I assessed the situation and realized that after nearly five years in the business, I was more than ready for this promotion. I applied for, and not surprisingly, was given the job. I was a couple months ahead of schedule as far as landing a job after college. The pay raise certainly didn't hurt either, especially with the growing number of mouths to feed at home!

In August of 2004, ironically on the day of my 10-year high school reunion (how's THAT for a ten-year plan?) I graduated from Southern Illinois University. Renea threw me a graduation party worthy of someone who spent ten years in college. Family and friends came from long distances to take part in the festivities. It was a magical day.

Things were going so well, in fact, that Renea and I started to kick around the idea of staying in Carbondale long term. We had great friends, good jobs, a nice house, albeit a bit small for the five animals...the only thing we didn't like was the area. Our neighborhood was nice, but the town of Carbondale was on the downslide, and it was very evident. Years later, the brother of one of our station photographers was tragically stabbed and killed in a senseless crime that remains unsolved today. It happened just blocks from our house, at a park where families bring their children and weekly summer concerts are held. We may have been living in what was dubbed as the "Professor's Barrio," but the fact that crimes like this were happening in our neighborhood showed that crime knows no boundaries and it was spreading like a wildfire in Carbondale.

We looked at new homes on the outskirts of Herrin, Illinois, which was the next town east of the TV station, which would amount to about a 10-minute commute for me and a 30-minute commute for Renea. We found a charming new neighborhood that was still under construction and placed a bid on a home currently being built. We hadn't sold our house yet, so the bid had a contingency based on the sale of our home. Before we even had our house on the market, another offer came in on the new construction. We realized what a pain it was going to be to try to buy and sell at the same time and decided to stay in Carbondale for the time being. The decision ended up being a blessing in disguise.

Chapter 8
The Power of Positivity

We survived day one of having a down dog at home. Technically it was only evening number one, and only a couple hours at that. I left the house the morning after bringing Keegan home not having a clue how we were going to survive the next days, weeks and months ahead trying to care for her, take proper care of our other pets, keep our marriage healthy and keep our sanity in the process.

On my way out the door I grabbed some of the literature our physical therapist gave us to review at work. One of the forms was an order form for a company called "Doggone Wheels." This company made wheelchairs for down dogs that allowed you to harness them in and gave them the ability to walk around with the rear part of their body in a sling attached to a wheeled cart. It was quite the contraption, but the photos of down dogs up and walking were inspiring. As if we hadn't spent enough money already, the cost of a chair for a dog Keegan's size was $400. Thank God for credit cards. Our physical therapist had taken all of Keegan's measurements in the event we wanted to order a wheelchair. I thought we'd wait and see how she did, but after having her home for less than 24 hours, the reality was setting in that it would be a long road to any type of recovery. I called that morning and ordered Keegan a "Doggone

Wheels" wheelchair. Cross that off the "phone calls I never thought I'd make" list.

I also found a website listed on one of the sheets given to us by our therapist, www.handicappedpets.com. I jumped online and began searching the site. There wasn't anything I hadn't already seen before; a lot of useful information on how to care for your pet, but it was material I had already printed out and shared with Renea. Then I stumbled across the message board. I noticed a section called "Paralyzed Pets" and clicked on it. From there, I found a post labeled "FCE," which was Keegan's official diagnosis. Click, click, click; I was going down a rabbit hole, hoping that the deeper I got the closer I would come to an answer for Keegan. I entered the FCE message string and read…and read…and read some more. I read each post with an incredulous gaze. They were nearly identical to ours, so much that you could replace Keegan's name with the other pet and our names with the other owners and the story would be a replica of our experience. What was more amazing was that many of the stories ended with their dogs walking again! *What is this, a cruel joke?* I thought.

The way the specialist laid things out to us, things looked pretty grim for Keegan. I didn't let myself get overly excited, but I was certainly curious. I read on for hours about all the different cases of down dogs from causes such as FCE, ruptured discs, and other incidents and accidents. Most had the same exposition, with a vet telling owners that the dog would never walk again. But they all had different resolutions. Some dogs recovered 100%; others regained the use of one of their legs, which enabled them to get up and limp around. Others learned to "spinal walk," which means they learned to beat the system and use their lifeless legs as props to help scoot across the ground. It didn't sound ideal in all cases, but one thing remained the same; all the owners offered unconditional love and support to their dogs to give them the best chance to recover.

After coming to this realization, I shifted my focus more towards how we should be acting towards Keegan and less on trying to figure out her chances of getting better. The recurring theme was to try to keep your down dog's life as normal as possible. Follow the same routines and maintain regular attitudes and behaviors. Most importantly, you must keep your own spirits up and not let your pet see that you are upset. I paid close attention to the success cases on the message board, and they all seemed to have that in common. I decided that this was the path we needed to take. It wouldn't be easy, that was certain, but for Keegan it was a necessity. I was trying so desperately to come up with a plan of action, and at the moment that consisted of…staying positive? It didn't seem like the greatest plan, but in entering this new world of down dogs and the community I discovered on the handicapped pets website, it seemed as logical a place to start as any.

It may sound primitive, but the message board was a godsend. This was before the era of smartphones and social media. The internet was still relatively in its infancy in comparison to today. There were resources online but not nearly as many as today, and making connections wasn't as easy as it is now, so stumbling across the message board and having access to the experiences of others was invaluable.

I did a little more searching throughout the day on the message board and forwarded the links to my home e-mail, so I could share the information with Renea. I returned from work with a much brighter attitude than when I left eight hours prior. Renea, however, was as glum as ever. I was anxious to tell her all about my newfound optimism, but she was more concerned with cleaning up Keegan's area. More pee awaited us in her bed, so I picked her up to get her outside. When I did, more pee drained out of her bladder and tricked down my pants and leg.

"Ok," I said calmly. "I've got more pee coming out here, and it's all over my leg." Renea laughed at that, and I was happy to hear the sound. "It's ok, girl," I told Keegan as we navigated past the bed and to the door.

More pee emptied out of her bladder, and by the time we finally did make it outside, she was pretty much finished. I continued feeling around for the bladder and finally found it. It felt just like they said it would, a little balloon that moved around. I squeezed on it, but nothing else came out. I took a beat sitting outside with Keegan, watching our cold breath exhale out of my mouth and her nose, while Renea threw the bedding in the washer and cleaned up all the pee.

Once we got Keegan back inside and situated, we turned our attention to getting our other dogs outside and fed. When that task was complete, it was time to start Keegan's physical therapy, which consisted of leg bends, balancing on a blow-up exercise ball, massage, and range of motion movements in bed. We hoisted her up with her sling and took her outside to pee before starting, just to be safe. I squeezed and squeezed, but nothing came out. When we got her inside and on the ball, however, we must have hit the sweet spot of the bladder (I believe there is such a thing now), because more pee came out. I wasn't even sure where she was keeping all of it!

"We've got more pee!" I said and lifted her up to get her back outside. This, of course, just sent more pee all over the floor. I hadn't yet realized that if I just let her pee, there would only be one spot to clean up. Moving her around in such a frantic fashion was just spraying pee all over the floor. Renea cleaned Keegan's area for the third time in an hour, and we set out to do her exercises for the second time.

Once we got her on the ball, I was finally able to tell Renea about some of the information I found on the handicappedpets.com message board. She wasn't buying it, not after the hour we'd just experienced. I tried to explain how important it was that we stay positive, but the last round of Keegan's accidents had pushed her over the edge. She didn't want to listen to anything I had to say, and I couldn't blame her. She was tired from getting little sleep the night before, exhausted physically and emotionally from the past few days, and after a full day's work we were now spending the entire night trying to care for our dog. It was all too much. I could tell the pressure was building and something was about to break. And I was right. By the time we finished Keegan's exercises, Renea broke.

She started bawling, still adjusting to our new life with a dog unable to do anything with the lower half of her body. The experience had left us feeling helpless and hopeless. Looking down at our beautiful dog who, just a week ago happy and healthy, was laying there with no use of her hindquarters, tail tucked between her legs and no bladder or bowel control; it was a devastating site. But after reading about all the success stories, I was determined to stay strong for Keegan. I just had to find a way to convince Renea to feel the same. I had been telling her all night about the dogs that walked again after going through what Keegs was battling, and how important it was that we stay strong and positive. Now, it was my turn to break.

"If you're going to do that, do it upstairs and not in front of Keegan," I said to Renea sternly.

I wasn't trying to be a jerk but didn't know how else to snap her out of her funk. I was desperately clinging to positivity as the only elixir to offer any relief to Keegan, and finding it was nearly impossible. It also didn't help that for the first time during this entire ordeal we had to muzzle Keegan. During all the prodding and probing, sleeping in veterinary kennels and even taken to St. Louis and left alone overnight, she had remained her sweet-natured self. No doubt sore from trying to carry all her weight on her front legs coupled with being hauled around by the vets and us had finally worn on her. When I moved her from the exercise ball to her bed, she snapped at me. I didn't scold her, in fact, I praised her for being so sweet for so long. But unfortunately, it also meant we had to muzzle her to finish the remaining exercises.

By the time we finished, Renea's tears had turned to sniffles. It was now 9 p.m. and we had just enough time and energy to have a quick bite to eat and go to bed. As we made dinner, I pulled the website up on the laptop computer and asked Renea to read some of the stories online. She finally agreed. By the end of the night, she was posting on the website herself. This is what she posted:

On 1/31/08, my husband found our Chow/Golden, Keegan, unable to move when he came home from lunch. He immediately took her to our vet. They ran tests and on Monday, referred us to a neurologist. We took her to a neurologist two hours away with hopes that the MRI would show something that was fixable with surgery. Unfortunately, the MRI showed that she has some sort of FCE around T-13, L-1. She is completely paralyzed from waist down, no feeling whatsoever. She cannot control her bladder. The vet said her prognosis is poor, however, said he would never count a dog out. We picked her up last night and needless to say it has been a rough 24 hours. We have ordered her a wheelchair. We did physical therapy with her last night and again today. We bought an orthopedic bed, diapers, etc. and have her in a comfortable place. We also have a sling to allow her to walk with her front legs a little bit. It is so hard to see her so limp in the back. She has been in pretty good spirits considering the circumstances, except tonight we had to muzzle her to do therapy. My husband has been on all of these sites and is optimistic about her recovery. I, on the other hand, am very depressed. I cry every time I am around her, although I try to hide it. I am stressed about the peeing everywhere, didn't sleep much, and feel overwhelmed. Are we doing right by her? Can she get better? How does everyone manage? I am exhausted and it's only been 24 hours. Please, I need real hope. Will the next weeks, months of sleepless nights, cleaning up, back aches, expenses of therapy, diapers, wheelchair, etc., etc. be worth it? She deserves a good life. She deserves so much more and I want to give her that, just feel overwhelmed. Help!

The feeling of despair still lingered, but after reading other peoples' stories on the web I could tell that Renea saw a small ray of light at the end of the tunnel that I found earlier in the day. More than anything in the world we wanted Keegan to walk again, and it appeared that to do so, we would have to stay upbeat, no matter how hard things got. I asked Renea if she was completely committed to doing so, and she agreed that for Keegan, there was no other option. We were bound and determined to get our girl walking again.

Keegan's Journal

January 31, 2008

Dear Diary,

Today Travis and Renea (my parents) found me unable to move. I was rushed to the veterinarian where I overheard my parents say that I suffered a spinal stroke. They also told me not to worry because they are staying positive and have a plan. If I could have wagged my tail I would have.

Chapter 9
The Miracle of Dr. Ava Frick

We have greed, it seems, to thank for advances in animal physical therapy. The unregulated sport of horse racing was booming at the end of the 19th century, but in the early 1900s most states had banned bookmaking. In 1908 just 25 race tracks were in operation in the U.S. However, the allure of cash was just too good for the government to pass up. When pari-mutuel betting (a system where those who bet on competitors finishing in the first three places share the total amount bet, minus percentage for management and taxes) was introduced at the 1908 Kentucky Derby, states saw the windfall opportunity. Many states legalized this type of gambling, and popularity of the sport of horse racing surged. More equine sporting events meant more injuries, and the field of veterinary rehabilitation expanded[9].

Sports would once again play a role in advancing the animal rehabilitation field in the 1980s. The International Racing Greyhound Symposium was started in 1986 and later renamed the International Canine Sports Medicine Symposium to include all

---

[9] Kentucky Derby. (n.d.). Kentucky Derby History. Retrieved from https://www.kentuckyderby.com/history/kentucky-derby-history

sporting dogs[10]. These symposiums served as a launching point for more research in canine rehabilitation. The additional interest in research, coupled with our growing love affair with house pets, led us to where we are today. Presently there are more than 110 facilities nationwide providing physical therapy and rehabilitation for animals, and the number is growing.

Dr. Ava Frick is one of the pioneers in the field of animal rehabilitation. As interest in the field grew, so did her accolades. Dr. Ava received her veterinary degree in 1980, a certification in Animal Chiropractic in 1997, and a proficiency certification in Herbal Phytotherapy in 2006. She is recognized as the world's leading veterinary authority in the application of microcurrent therapy for animals. Her accomplishments are lengthy; published author, member of the Animal Chiropractic Hall of Fame, national lecturer, and noted researcher. But most important for us, *she* was the doctor we would put every ounce of our faith and trust in to find a way to get Keegan walking again.

Day two with a down dog began with me searching for therapy options. I had concerns that the original plan of massage and range of motion exercises wouldn't be enough to get Keegan on her feet again, so I did more digging on my own. The previous day, I educated myself on what exactly FCE was and if there was any chance of recovery for Keegan. Now that I knew she had a shot at improvement it was time to find out the best way to do that.

As I read more of peoples' stories online, I began to see a pattern of what seemed to connect all the dogs that recovered. For one, the owners were all 100% committed to their animal's recovery. Like,

---

[10] Doctor of Veterinary Medicine 360. (2009). Canine Rehabilitation: An Inside Look at a Fast-Growing Market Segment. Retrieved from http://veterinarynews.dvm360.com/canine-rehabilitation-inside-look-fast-growing-market-segment

crazy committed. That meant no matter what, Keegan comes first over the needs of Renea and me, and unfortunately over our other animals. We could worry about making it up to them later, but for now, it was going to be all Keegan, all the time. I could live with that.

Second, it appeared that some serious rehab was needed, asap. As I suspected, this meant more than the simple exercises we were currently doing. We're talking about some hardcore therapy involving hydrotherapy with an underwater treadmill, among other things. "The sooner you can get your dog into rehab, the better," was the urging from owners of all successfully rehabbed down dogs. There was a problem with this scenario. We lived in Quincy, which is a small town of about 40,000 people. There isn't exactly a booming market for animal rehabilitation services. I expanded my search to nearby Springfield, Illinois and St. Louis. It was after expanding my search that I came across Dr. Ava.

It was by chance when doing a web search for "St. Louis pet therapy" that I found an archived article that had appeared in the *St. Louis Post-Dispatch*. The story stopped short of calling Dr. Ava a miracle worker but professed she could do just about everything *but* miracles. I quickly located her website and began scouring the site for information.

According to her biography, Dr. Ava initially began her career as a conventional practitioner specializing in rabbits. Later, she transitioned to chiropractic and animal rehabilitation. In 1997, she became interested in human physical therapy applications and how they could be used to treat animals, including household pets and large animals such as horses and alpacas.

Dr. Ava started her business long before the current fad of pampering our animals with massages and spa treatments. At the time her rehab facilities were based in Union, Mo., about 45 minutes southwest of St. Louis. *This is a possibility* I said to myself. Three hours is quite a haul, but if it meant getting Keegs into rehab, I would figure something out.

I was amazed at all the different treatment options listed on the website. First, there was the hydrotherapy that everyone on the handicappedpets.com website championed. There was also chiropractic, acupuncture, electronic stimulus, and nutrition services. The impressive array of rehab options paired with the *Post-Dispatch* endorsement was everything I needed to be convinced. I clicked the contact button on Dr. Ava's website and sent an e-mail describing Keegan's condition and asked if she thought Keegan would be a favorable patient for therapy. I was brimming with hope and excitement for myself, Renea, and most important, Keegan.

Renea and I met at the house on coordinated lunch breaks on day two to get Keegan outside to pee and back inside for exercises. I took her out and expressed her bladder at 7:30 a.m. before I left for work. It was now 12:30, five hours later. We were trying to limit the amount of water she drank when we weren't home, but it was hard to tell if we were giving her enough because a side effect of a medication she was on to prevent bladder infections was, of course, excessive thirst. Not exactly helping our pee problem.

We were delighted and surprised to find Keegan in a dry bed, but as soon as I lifted her up with the sling, out came the pee, all over my leg and shoes.

"Here we go again," I said. Renea laughed as I stood calmly with pee all over my pants.

I'm not what you could call the most patient person in the world, and usually overreact to small problems. My non-reaction was quite a surprise to Renea. It was only the second time I heard her laugh since her birthday. If Keegan peeing on me was what it took, so be it.

We eventually got her outside to finish her pee, but unfortunately, there was still no sign of poop. She had been home for two days now, and although the peeing was plentiful, I was concerned about the lack of a bowel movement. Now it was my turn to laugh. Things that used to gross me out were now being discussed in casual tones. We felt like we had a newborn baby at home and had no idea what to do with it. *The baby isn't pooping, what do we do?*

Once we got Keegan inside and situated, I told Renea all about Dr. Ava and the rehab facility in Union. She wasn't quite as excited as I was, but agreed that if Keegan needed professional rehab, St. Louis was a possibility. I couldn't wait to hear back from the doctor, so once I got back to work (with a clean pair of pants and different shoes), I called the facility to see how soon we could get her in. I was greeted by a friendly voice that listened to my description of Keegan's condition and informed me that yes, Dr. Ava could work with us to help Keegan's situation. It was now Thursday, and the earliest they could get Keegan in was the following Tuesday. I explained that we were driving down from Quincy and it was about three hours, so we wouldn't be able to do the preferable every other day schedule. She told me that many times people leave their dogs for a week to do more intensive therapy with Dr. Ava, but we would need to discuss that with her once Keegan was examined.

It wasn't until later that night when working with Keegan that Renea and I both realized that we just got her back from the specialist on Tuesday, and we may have to leave her with another doctor in a few days. We had only been working with her for two days. Even though it was exhausting and felt like a month already, the thought of not having her at home again was breaking both our hearts. Something else was breaking our hearts, too, though. We had two dogs upstairs desperate for our attention. It was attention we simply didn't have the time to give them.

There was something else we were running out of quickly: money. In fact, we weren't running out; we were already there. We put everything we could, including gas for the trips to St. Louis and all the food, treats and supplies, on our debit card so it would come straight from our checking account. The big vet bills had to go on a credit card. Financially, things had been going well up until now. We had curbed any unnecessary spending and were resolved to get rid of our credit card debt to focus on student loans. Then, in the heart of that effort, the incident with Keegan happened. Throw the current plan out the window.

Renea and I had both been so overcome with shock and emotion after Keegan first went down that we didn't really care what the financial costs were for her diagnosis and, we were praying, her eventual recovery. Now, a week after her spinal stroke and with current bills coming due and an expensive rehab looming in the future, the financial reality of the situation was setting in. In two words, Renea, who handled all our finances, summed up our situation.

"I'm not sure what to do," she said. "We're screwed."

We both agreed that Keegan's trip to Union for an assessment and hopefully scheduled rehab by Dr. Ava was a must. How we would pay for it was another matter. We both had small amounts saved up in retirement funds, but not enough to bail us out of trouble. Besides, the penalties and fees associated with early withdrawals weren't worth it in the long run. Our plan to get out of debt meant putting everything we could each payday towards our bills, so we didn't have a savings built up. We did have one more option, however. A giant house we could sell. How did we end up with a giant house? A recent move from Carbondale to Quincy came with a new addition to the household: Jedi.

Chapter 10
Return of the Jedi

In November of 2004, we visited friends and family in Quincy for Thanksgiving. Karma filled the atmosphere as all our old friends happened to get together over the weekend. Renea and I both agreed that although we were happy in Carbondale, something was missing. We felt this was what it was; the camaraderie we shared with our closest old friends and our family nearby.

"This is what it's all about," I said to our old friends sitting together at a restaurant. "We miss you guys, a lot."

I talked to a few of my old co-workers who were still at WGEM, and casually asked them to let me know if something became available in Quincy. There were only two television stations in Quincy, which limited my job opportunities. There were a few colleges in the area, but the small population meant little turnover, limiting Renea's options as well. We were both well qualified in our fields, but having the right situation come open in Quincy would be the challenge.

We returned to our lives in Carbondale after the holiday with the intention to keep things status quo but leave our options open for jobs elsewhere. We had a great group of friends and our family of dogs and cats was a nice balance. Keegan and Canada got along great, and Bud pretty much slept all the time. Cha and P.J. were inseparable, and Akili was the princess of the group. People were always surprised at how well our animals co-existed. That was until one fateful December day.

Renea called me at work and told me she just took in a dog that was running down the street with a broken chain attached to his collar. She described him as a beautiful but dirty black lab with long hair. I asked her to keep him in the kitchen separated from the other dogs, and we'd decide what to do next when I got home after the ten o'clock newscast. Sure enough, I arrived home to find a filthy, shaggy black dog dirtying up our kitchen. But Renea was right; he was a beautiful dog. He was sweet-natured but showed quite a bit of trepidation towards us, which we didn't like. Whenever we would try to pet him, he would duck his head down, as if we were going to strike him. We chalked it up to him scared of being away from home and in a new place full of strange people and animals. We pushed our table into the corner and gave him a large dog bed to lie down on through the night. The next day we would begin the search for his owners.

Renea asked around the neighborhood and told the mailman that if he knew of anyone missing a dog, it's probably the one at our house. We had no luck after one day and kept him overnight for a second night. That evening we began discussing what to do if no one claimed him. We already had a full house, a fact that wasn't up for debate. We decided there was simply no way we could keep the lab. We would begin searching for a new home for him if his owners couldn't be found.

We never had to start that process, however, as the mailman informed Renea the next day that he found the owners. They lived a few blocks from us and would be down that afternoon to pick him up. I wasn't there when they arrived, but Renea's encounter did not sit well with either of us. The family did not look like the kind of family you would want to turn any animal over to.

"Looks like we'll have to get a heavier chain," they said gruffly as they led the lab back to their car.

No "thank you" to Renea for finding their dog, keeping him for two nights, and tracking them down. She was standing there on our front porch with the broken chain in her hand and a heavy heart. They drove away with the lab and Renea went back inside and shut herself in the bathroom, where she cried for a good five minutes. She knew something was not right with this situation.

In the following weeks, we would walk or drive by their house and see him tied to a tree in the backyard with a chain. It did not matter if it was raining or snowing, he was always outside tied to that tree. Then we thought back to the way he cowered from us when we tried to pet him, and it didn't take long to realize this dog was being denied a fair shot. We talked about our options. We could steal the dog. We weren't thieves, specifically animal thieves. Besides, how do you steal a dog from people two blocks from your house? You can't exactly hide him. We discussed offering to buy the dog from them, but if they refused, we could never hatch another plan to rescue him. It would be obvious who the culprits were. We couldn't come up with a viable option and were still kicking around the idea of offering to buy him when the impossible happened. He showed back up on our doorstep.

A historic snow and ice storm hit southern Illinois just before Christmas, and the conditions were brutal. The ice came first, coating everything with about a half inch of ice around midnight. More than a foot of snow followed in the early morning hours. The interstate leading into the area was shut down for three days. Power lines across the region had snapped. A day after the storm hit, I received a phone call from Renea shortly after arriving at the station, around 2 p.m.

"Holy crap, he's back," she said.

"Who?" I asked, puzzled.

"The dog, the lab from down the street. He broke his chain again and came to our front door!" she exclaimed.

I might not have believed this story myself had she not offered the photographic proof. Not only did the dog break his chain for a second time, but he also returned to our house and parked his butt on our porch, staring down our front door. Our dogs had started barking wildly, and Renea jumped up to see what all the commotion was. There he was, sitting calmly on the porch. If he knew how to knock on the door, that would have been his next move. She ran into the bedroom, grabbed the camera, and snapped a picture from the window. Next, she put Keegan, Canada and Bud in separate rooms and ran to the door to let our frozen new friend inside.

Return of the Jedi

Again, she cobbled together a living area for him in our kitchen, and then called me. I still wasn't 100% convinced of her story until I returned home on my dinner break. Remember, this was before the era of smart phones, so she couldn't just instantly send me a photo. I had to see it to believe it. Indeed, there he was, sitting in our kitchen with a grateful look in his eyes. It didn't even need to be said, Renea and I both knew there was no way we were going to return the dog a second time. He arrived literally with ice hanging off his shaggy coat. It was obvious he had been left outside during the record-setting storm. This was our chance to make up for our first mistake of returning him to such a lousy home. It was almost as if he sensed we'd already decided to rescue him because his mood was somehow different this time around. He just collapsed into us when we sat with him in the kitchen, discussing what to do next.

The first thing we decided on was his name. He returned to us in amazing fashion, that much couldn't be denied. Because of this, I thought the name "Jedi" was very fitting, referring to the *Star Wars* movie, *Return of the Jedi*. Renea loved it, and Jedi was born. With the black lab serving as the unlikely accomplice, we achieved the first part of our goal, which was to somehow reacquire the dog now known as Jedi. What now?

I came up with a plan that was risky but gave us the best of chance of keeping Jedi for good. The first time he came up missing, we had him for two days and the owners, who lived two short blocks away, did nothing to try to find him. We had to find them. I had them pegged as the type of people who would just replace a missing dog rather than go through the trouble of searching for him. He wasn't neutered, spent the first part of his life (length still undetermined at this point) tied to a tree, and had gone missing before.

My plan was to turn him into the local animal shelter as a lost dog and inform them that we would adopt him if he wasn't claimed in the required seven-day wait period given to lost dogs. It was a plan fraught with pitfalls. First, I could have been wrong about the owners making a simple call to the pound. Second, the shelter was not "no-kill," so if he got lost in the system and they forgot to call us to adopt, he would most likely be put to sleep. Finally, it was just hard to give him up again after he so blatantly showed up at our doorstep looking for shelter and love. The implausible way he returned to us had me re-thinking everything I thought I knew about animals. His behavior showed a display of memory and rational, critical thinking. The image of him sitting on our doorstep is one that will continue to astonish me until the day I go to the grave.

Keeping him outright, however, meant always looking over our shoulder waiting for his previous owners to see him in our yard or see us out on a walk with him. We wanted to keep Jedi and give him the loving, safe home he had been denied, but we wanted to do it the right way. We weighed our options and decided that in the long run, the legal adoption process was the best way to go. The next day we made the difficult call to the animal warden to report a "lost dog."

The animal control officer showed up a few hours later to take Jedi to the shelter. We gave him our information with the explicit instructions to have the shelter contact us in seven days. We probably told him ten times that we knew he would be put to sleep if he wasn't claimed and that we wanted to keep him but wanted to give the owners a chance to claim him first (knowing full well they wouldn't go looking for him). He just nodded his head each time we told him. This time, I joined Renea in crying when the officer pulled away from our house, with a confused Jedi in the back of his truck.

We spent Christmas in Carbondale and went to Quincy for two days after the holiday to see family and friends with an interesting story about Jedi to share with them. As soon as we returned to Carbondale, at the five-day mark of his chance to be claimed, we called the shelter to make sure he was still there. It was no surprise when they identified the black lab we reported lost. It was also no surprise when the worker informed us there were no notes in his file about us wanting to adopt him after the seven-day period. We assured them we did and asked for our information to be put in his file while we waited on the phone.

The shelter was closed on the seventh day because of the New Year holiday. We called on January 2nd to find out if he had been claimed (we already knew the answer to that). We weren't expecting what came next. They put the manager of the shelter on the phone, and she informed us that he was still there, but we probably didn't want to adopt him. Her bluntness was not a surprise. When we adopted Canada from the same shelter two years earlier, we were met with rude service and the attitude that we were somehow doing something wrong by rescuing a dog from the shelter. I understand how people in charge of animal shelters can easily become jaded. I can't imagine the amount of animal abuse and neglect they deal with, and I know they want the best possible home for each and every animal that comes through the shelter doors. I'm sure after time the lines become blurred and you become suspicious of every person or couple who wants to adopt from the shelter.

Jedi had been full of energy in the short time we had him, so I assumed she was going to try to talk me out of adopting such a wild dog. Unfortunately, that was not the case. A standard heartworm test that they give to all incoming dogs at the shelter came up positive; Jedi had stage two heartworms. There are only three stages of heartworm total, with the last equaling death. It made sense that he had heartworms. He was left outside through the summer months, and one would have to assume his neglectful owners did not have him on any type of heartworm protection. And so, the plot thickened.

After all the worrying and protecting we had done for Jedi, there was no way we could let him down now. We asked the shelter manager what the next step would be if we wanted to get him treatment. Much to our dismay, we learned that heartworm treatments are expensive and very difficult for both dog and owner. A series of shots injected into the spine introduces the toxin meant to kill the worms. The dead worms can dislodge and cause blood clots in an animal's lungs, so a dog undergoing treatment should be kennel-bound for sixty days. This is meant to keep them as still as possible, making it less likely for the dead worms to lodge in the lungs.

The manager was quite surprised by our decision to go forward with the adoption and agreed to make the appointment with a local vet as soon as possible to begin treatment. With that, we could come in the next day to pick him up. Despite the unexpected diagnosis, we were beyond relieved. The entire time we thought about him in that cold shelter, wondering why we didn't keep him safe, why we turned him over to the authorities. Unfortunately, there's no way to explain to animals why you do what you do to keep them out of harm's way. We were so afraid he would get lost in the shuffle and euthanized after no one claimed him. Finally, after more than a week of anxiously waiting, we were able to pick up Jedi and adopt him legally as our own. We started heartworm treatments that week, and thankfully it wasn't too late. We purchased the largest kennel we could find and set him up in our bedroom. We figured that would be the best place to keep him where he could still be around us and away from the other dogs. We had doctor's orders to keep him as still as possible but quickly found out that was going to be a challenge. The vet estimated Jedi to be two years old. Have you ever met a two-year-old lab? They're quite the bundle of energy. We also began to see more of the abused dog come out in him. For one, he wasn't trained as an indoor pet to go outside to relieve himself, having spent the first two years of his life tied to a tree. He wouldn't poop in his kennel, but he would pee whenever he wanted to because the kennel was a wire frame and he could just lift his leg and pee outside of the kennel. When we scolded him the first time he did it, he became a different dog, growling and snapping at us. We didn't know what to do, having never been around a dog that was violent towards us. We had sixty days to figure it out.

Before Jedi's sixty-day sentence was up, something else very big happened. A good friend and former co-worker at WGEM remembered what I told him the past Thanksgiving and called one morning the following February to say the evening producer was moving to Madison, Wisconsin, and I should talk to the news director about the job. I immediately called the newsroom, and the news director was already awaiting my phone call. I set up an interview for that Friday, and by the following Monday, I accepted the job offer. After several years, our journey was taking us back to Quincy.

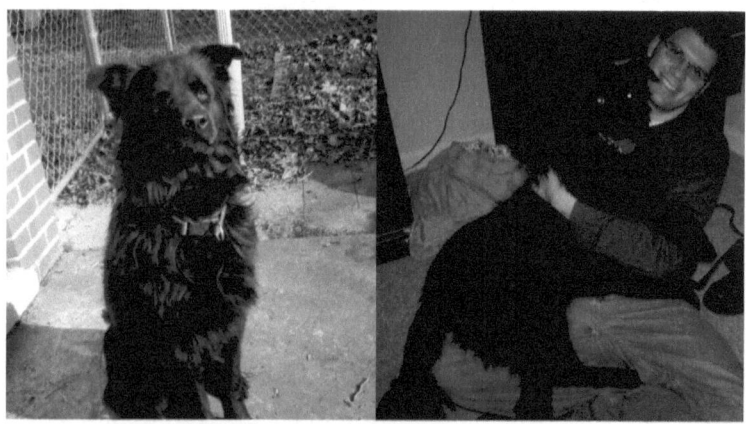

Jedi before and after his adoption

Chapter 11
Let There Be Poop

After finally deciding that Keegan's veterinary and rehab bills were going to put us over the top financially, we began searching for a house that would cost considerably less than our current home in Quincy. We scheduled a meeting with a realtor, and she thought she could sell our home for $20,000 more than what we paid for it. That, coupled with the money we'd already paid on the house, would be enough to get us out of debt and back on track. It was not an easy decision. Leaving our current home was tough to think about. We had been in the house for three years, and in that time, we remodeled every room, including busting a wall out in the basement to create a giant family room. We also raided K's Merchandise, a Midwest retail chain, when they went out of business. We got a beautiful couch and chair set and a dining room set for a fraction of the cost. New carpet in the living room and basement, new flooring in the dining room, and new paint in every room were just some of the improvements we'd been busy with. Frankly, there wasn't much left to remodel. We finally got it where we wanted it, and now we had to leave. We both continued to flip-flop on the idea. One day I would be excited about the prospect of being much more financially stable, while Renea hated the idea of leaving our home. The next day, it would be my turn to be depressed while she got excited about the prospect of financial freedom. We continued back and forth while we searched the homes available.

Selling a house full of animals is just one of the many challenges we faced. We did this when we moved from Carbondale, and it was a nightmare. Now, not only did we have the animals, but a handicapped dog in the basement that wasn't exactly mobile. We could pick a day of the week to show the house and kennel the animals, but that limited the visibility of our home and the number of people looking at it. We also couldn't kennel Keegan, and after everything she had been through I wasn't about to make her spend a full day in the vet's office every week.

Our other option was a bridge loan, which would solve all the animal problems, but also came with the risk of having two house payments for an undetermined amount of time. We went this route when we sold our home in Carbondale, and had two mortgages for three months, a very stressful time both mentally and to our bank account. We couldn't afford another financial crisis like that, so we decided we'd have to kennel the animals and just keep Keegan in the house. It would be stressful on her, but not nearly as bad as the alternative.

The next problem was finding a home cheap enough that would still meet our needs. We needed space, first and foremost; anything less than a thousand square feet and we would most likely be tripping over each other and the animals. Next, we had to have a yard for the dogs. If it wasn't fenced in, we just added on an additional $2,000 to the cost of the home, as it was a project that would have to be done before we moved in. The neighborhood was just as important, if not more, than the house itself. You can renovate a home, but once a neighborhood goes, there's no going back. We currently lived in a subdivision on the edge of town and loved the quiet setting and privacy. Odds were, we would find something in town along one of the main roads. We didn't want to narrow the search parameters to the point where nothing was available, so we decided on three factors: Price, size and neighborhood. Anything too pricy made the move a moot point; anything too small would probably signal the end of our sanity and possibly even our marriage; we'd use discretion when sizing up the neighborhood but knew we'd have to downgrade.

This new development made the cost of Keegan's impending rehab a bit more bearable. We were now looking forward to her potential intensive rehab in St. Louis and the idea of a couple days free of early morning and late-night rehab. We made it to Friday, surviving the first week with a down dog. The weekend, however, brought its own challenges. I was a bit scared to be home all day. Going to work was a necessity, and I didn't feel bad neglecting Keegan while she hung out all day in the basement by herself. With Saturday and Sunday all to ourselves, what would we do? How could I relax upstairs knowing she was downstairs in her bed unable to get up and move around? It seemed that no matter the situation, Keegan's stroke added multiple levels of physical and mental challenges.

Friday also brought a few blessings to us. First, things had gotten a bit easier thanks to settling into our new routine. We developed a system of taking Keegan outside on the sling, switching all her bedding and then doing her exercises. That helped a lot. Keegan seemed to be settling into her new situation as well. She still wasn't happy about it, but our prescription of tons of love and treats appeared to keep her spirits up. She had always been an antsy dog by nature, scared easily by strange sounds and loud noises. Renea thought having some background noise would help and decided on the 1960s XM radio channel on our satellite. It was happy and upbeat and would now become the ambient soundtrack to this part of

Keegan's life. Renea & I had very different musical tastes. I was a seventies man. My father was a program director at a radio station in the '70s and '80s, so I was raised on Billy Joel, Elton John, Michael McDonald, a lot of Yacht Rock. Renea preferred country, which was near the bottom of my musical preferences. It was only fitting that now our dog had a preference of her own. At least we hoped she did. To find out later that she hates '60s music would make me feel terrible! How does a dog tell you she hates a specific genre of music? Oh, the questions you ask yourself when you have a down dog.

Second, a celebration was in order. We finally got a bowel movement out of her Friday night. When stocking up on supplies earlier in the week, we picked up some rubber gloves just in case we had to…erm, I'll just call it what it is…manually stimulate her anus. Unfortunately, with no poop since at least Wednesday, we decided to try to get things moving on our own accord. I read about expressing a dog's bladder and anus and printed out the sheets for us for reference. Luckily for me, Renea volunteered for the job. While we balanced Keegan on the exercise ball, Renea slapped on a rubber glove, squirted a stream of water on the butt, and did a little massaging with her gloved hand. In about 30 seconds, we had a bowel movement. We were more happy than disgusted; in fact, besides the smell, we weren't bothered at all, happy even! I was starting to realize how new parents change diapers without much complaint. We laughed for a minute, praised Keegan on her accomplishment, and I bagged up the poop while Renea wiped the mat. We were now what you could call a well-oiled poop inducing machine.

Saturday morning, I woke up around 7:30 and went downstairs to take Keegan outside. We'd had a pretty bad winter already, and more snow had fallen overnight. Keegan loved the snow, so I took her out in the backyard, following behind with her rear end in the sling. She took off running with her front legs and launched her nose into the snow piled up next to the fence. From there, her snow-covered head popped up and looked around, then disappeared back into the snow. It was freezing, I was in pajama pants and slippers, traipsing around my snow-filled backyard with a dog in a sling, and I couldn't have been happier. Keegan would run about ten feet and then continue her snowy search along the fence line. All I could think about was following the advice to keep a down dog's life as normal as possible. Well, this was pretty typical for Keegan. In fact, it was just another winter morning for her. Only this time she had the entire yard to herself (not counting me, who she didn't seem to notice) and didn't have to deal with her pesky canine brother and sister. I followed along laughing as she circled the entire perimeter of the fence, stopping every ten to twenty feet to investigate what was beneath the fluffy white stuff.

When coming in from her romp, she led me from the back patio straight into the house and made a beeline for her bed. She plopped down on the bed with what I took as a strange sense of satisfaction. I kicked off my slippers, shook the snow off my pant legs, closed the door, tossed the sling and crawled onto the bed with her. I fixed her legs so they weren't tangled up and angled the electric heater towards us for some extra warmth on the cold winter morning.

We had survived the first couple days, came up with a system, and managed to keep Keegan's spirits up. Her KONG toy was a huge help. She would spend hours trying to lick the peanut butter and treats from the inside of the rubber contraption. I liked having goals to look forward to; it kept things manageable. The next goal to accomplish was getting to Tuesday's meeting with Dr. Ava in St. Louis. We kept our hopes up that the meeting would go well and Keegs would be considered a candidate for rehab.

Saturday was a balance of cleaning, relaxing upstairs and spending time downstairs with Keegan. It wasn't as hard as I thought it would be, and between Renea and me, we kept everyone in the house satisfied. The sun was out in the afternoon, so we took a blanket out into the driveway and brought Keegan out to lie in the sun for a while. She was excited and distracted by squirrels, birds, and the blowing wind. We often joke that like most retrievers, she has a touch of attention deficit disorder. I mean, who gets distracted by the wind? We finally coaxed her to lay still by bringing a chew treat out. When it was time to go inside, I lifted her up with her sling, and she began to pee. Then something exciting happened; she pooped on her own.

We couldn't believe it and started dancing around the driveway. Renea did most of the dancing; I still had Keegs in the sling and sort of just moved around like a grocery bagger having a seizure. It must have been quite a sight watching two grown adults and a dog in a sling, hopping around the driveway excitedly yelling about poop. But there we were, celebrating Keegan's big bowel movement.

"She pooped!" Renea yelled.

"Holy crap!" I exclaimed.

"Look at it!" Renea continued.

"You pooped!" I yelled, leaning down to show Keegan my excitement as if she couldn't tell I was excited from my yelling.

We watched on with joy as she went "number two" on her own. We were happy first for health reasons. We were already running the risk of a bladder infection because she couldn't pee on her own. I had no idea what to worry about if she couldn't poop. And of course, we were ecstatic that this meant we might not have to "massage the anus" every day. It was a joyous moment indeed.

We were excited about her pooping on her own, and lately, we'd noticed some small, almost minuscule, twitches in her leg muscles when tickling her paw pads and in between her pads, something I called "twinkle-toes" and had made a part of our daily rehab. I was anxious for Keegan's trip to see Dr. Ava and e-mailed her the update before we came down.

> Friday, February 8, 2008
> Dr. Frick,
> We've had Keegan home since Tuesday and have been doing range of motion exercises and movement on the exercise ball twice a day. Last night and this morning there seems to be much more "twitching" in her legs when tickling her pads. We're hoping this is a good sign. Keegan and I look forward to meeting with you on Wednesday!
>
> Friday, February 8, 2008
> Travis
> Thank you for the update. All sounds promising.
> Expect to be here a couple hours.
>
> Dr. Ava

We needed all the postive signs we could take, so I forwarded the e-mail to Renea, and we waited anxiously for Tuesday's appointment in Union, Missouri.

Keegan's Journal

February 13, 2008

Dear Diary,

It has been a rough month. I am unable to control my bowels. I go whenever everything fills up. It is very embarrassing and leaves quite a mess for Mom and Dad to clean up. They are very smart & clever; they wrapped both my beds in plastic and laid blankets. So when I do have an accident they only have to wipe down the plastic and swap blankets. I still can't feel anything past my shoulders, but I am getting by. I am going to see Dr. Frick today. Mom and Dad said that the ride would be long (4 hours) but it would be worth it. They have told me so much about her that I can't wait see her. I know that she has lots of things that will help me get better. I will write and tell you how it all goes.

Chapter 12
Not Ready for Rehab

Tuesday morning around eleven Renea, Keegan and I pulled out of the driveway, hopeful that good news and some good fortune was waiting for us in Union. The town of Union is about 45 miles southwest of St. Louis, and in looking at a map, it appeared there was no easy way to get there. Remember this was long before the days when GPS was readily available on every mobile device, so I turned to Mapquest.com to get the best route. Usually, I'd navigate myself using a standard road atlas, but I was in no mood to find shortcuts and random routes through the winding hills of Missouri. All was fine until we turned off Interstate 70. The roads twisted and turned, two miles on one road, five miles on another. Four-way stop, left for another three miles then turn right onto…you get the idea. Our last two trips to Dr. Holt's office in St. Louis were met with fog and rain. This day offered up perfect driving weather, but horrible directions that took us through what appeared to be every one-horse town between St. Louis and Union.

We finally came to a town with more than a bait shop and gas station, which surely had to be Union. Nope, this was Washington. We used to have an atlas in our car and SUV, but for some reason on this day the one in the SUV seemed to have disappeared. All we had to go on was tiny, blurred, printed directions complete with a map in a little box on the page so small it seemed built for a Smurf.

"Where are we?" I asked incredulously.

"I can't tell!" Renea fired back. "This crappy map only shows Union."

"Where's the damn atlas?" I asked to no one in particular.

Renea usually drove the car and I the SUV, so technically we were in "my" vehicle. I hadn't been in my right mind for almost two weeks now, so trying to locate the atlas mid-trip was a bigger task than either of us could handle. Renea tried. She awkwardly twisted around to rummage around the back through a tiny space left from the folded down seats, to no avail. We were running late, Keegan had been prone in the back going on three hours, and Renea and I were at each other's throats. She gave up on her search, and I labored down the highway. It was one of those trips you just wanted…needed…to end. Finally, like the mythical City Upon a Hill, or a unicorn leaping over a rainbow, the town of Union appeared.

We exhaled, and somehow miraculously we were only about 15 minutes late. Via our blurry little map, we navigated through town as best we could and eventually came to the turn that led to the rehab facility. It was more of a ranch type setup, with a white picket fence in the front, a steel building just off the road, and a giant barn behind the main building with a gravel road winding throughout, ending at a house set back behind the entire complex. Horses grazed in a giant pasture sitting just north of the small parking lot.

"We made it, Keegs!" I said, unbuckling and jumping out of the truck.

We stretched our legs and then opened the back hatch. Keegan was excited and pulled herself to the open door with her front legs. I lifted her from the truck and down into the waiting sling, then walked her around the driveway to stretch her legs while Renea went inside to check us in. Keegan smelled all the different animals and hopped around with her front legs all over the place. I took her to the side of the building and expressed her bladder before heading into the building that I hoped would be the place she took her first steps.

The inside was reminiscent of a lodge, with earth tones on the walls, wood beams on the ceiling, and a calming, soft music playing over house speakers. It was all very relaxing and inviting. I noticed photos on the wall of success stories; dogs that Dr. Ava helped rehabilitate, and wished so badly that Keegan would someday be on that wall with them.

I sat Keegan down in front of one of the chairs in the middle of the lobby and plopped down in the next chair, exhausted. Rest didn't last long. Keegan started fidgeting and then peed on the floor.

"Oh crap, sorry!" I said to no one and rushed outside with Keegan.

We walked around for a while, me blindly following behind with sling around her hindquarters as she sniffed away at everything she could find.

"Come on, sweetie; you have to pee," I told her.

We found some bushes, and it looked like as good a spot as any, so I dropped the sling and started squeezing around her belly again. Finally, a tiny squirt of pee came out.

"Is that it?" I asked her.

She gave me a look that said, *wouldn't you like to know*. I know this side of Keegan, the troublemaking side. While I was glad to see her injury hadn't taken part of her personality away from her, really all I wanted at that point was a quality bathroom break.

I acquiesced and went back inside, thanking the receptionist for cleaning up the mess. I wasn't back in the chair two minutes before another surprise came: It was time to poop.

"Ok, that's it!" I said, hopping out of my seat again. "Just come get us when the doctor is ready!" I hooked the sling back under Keegs, and back out we went.

"Sorry," Renea said as we headed out the door. She kept apologizing for Keegan as if they were in cahoots.

"No need to apologize," I said on my way out the door.

Unfortunately for the poor receptionist, Keegan did all her pooping inside and had nothing left by the time we got outside. Keegan was obviously nervous, so I decided I would try to wear her out. We weren't quite running around the parking lot, more like Keegan awkwardly hopping while I tried to keep up behind. I think the whole ordeal wore *me* out more than her. After a few minutes, Renea called from the door and said they were ready for Keegan.

Before seeing the doctor, a vet tech gave us a tour of the main building. It included an exercise room, observation rooms, a kennel area and a giant hydrotherapy tank. The entire place was very impressive and smelled clean, which is always a chore when animals are your business. We were led down a hallway to one of the observation rooms when Keegan was met by Cheerio, a cute little brown and white corgi. Cheerio was about a third of Keegan's size, but Keegan's sweet nature showed again as she just bent down and faced the new dog nose-to-nose, sniffing away.

"That's Cheerio," the vet tech informed us.

"Hi, Cheerio," I said as we continued past. I assumed Cheerio was the house dog because she seemed to have the run of the place.

We settled into a bright white observation room with colorful paintings on the wall and a small dish with bone-shaped treats in it. It was shaping up to be the antithesis of our experience with Dr. Holt. I snagged a couple of treats from the dish and offered them to Keegan. Evoking her inner Scooby Doo, no matter how nervous she got, she would always take time for a treat.

Renea and I sat patiently, all our hopes for Keegan passing silently between each other. Nothing needed to be said aloud. After so much time researching, looking for any reason to be hopeful of Keegan's prognosis, exhausted from running through the full gamut of emotions, the moment of truth was here.

Dr. Ava walked into the room and introduced herself. She appeared to be in her early 50's with a kind face and shoulder length curly blonde hair. She knelt and met Keegan for the first time. We recapped her injury, what we were doing rehab-wise, and gave her the X-rays done by our doctor in Quincy. We sat back as Dr. Ava poked and prodded Keegan to get a feel for where she was recovery-wise.

"That's not good," she said, pointing to her rear paws that were folded over. "She's knuckling. That's never good in a dog."

Renea and I shot each other worried glances. That was not what we were hoping to hear. Dr. Ava finished her examination and told us that Keegan wasn't strong enough to stay for intensive rehab yet. I clung to the *yet* part as we hung on her every word, hoping and praying for positive news. She saved the best for last.

"There are lots of exercises you can do to build up her strength," she continued. "I'll walk you through them, and we'll prescribe some vitamins and medications that will also help build her system back up. We'll reevaluate in ten days, but she should be ready by then."

There was the news we were hoping for! I decided to lay it all out on the table then and there and asked what she thought about Keegan making a full recovery. She explained that the owners play a big role in a dog's recovery. She praised us for the work we had been doing so far.

"Keegan is lucky to have two wonderful owners, and I think she can recover fully," she told us. "We'll put her in the underwater treadmill before you leave today, and we'll see how we do in ten days."

Dr. Ava showed us all kinds of new exercises to do with Keegan. For starters, the exercise ball prescribed by the initial therapist was way too large. It seemed very awkward every time we used it, and now we understood why. There was also a full body vest that Keegan could wear full-time that was much better for carrying down dogs around than the sling we'd been using. I was quickly realizing the empty feeling we had when we left Dr. Holt's office for the last time was more than justified. Caring for a paralyzed dog had to be more than a 30-minute training session and a "good luck, see you later." Apparently, I was right.

Dr. Ava went to work on Keegan and we saw instant results. Up to this point the only movement we saw in her legs was tiny twitches from doing the "twinkle-toes" exercise. Dr. Ava showed us web pulls, where you pull the dog's leg straight, holding on to the web in between the toes until the leg jerks back. Keegan showed a great response to these, with her legs reacting nearly every time Dr. Ava pulled. After so much time seeing no movement from her back legs...this it was our turn to nearly have an accident in the doctor's facility.

"Oh my god!" Renea said. "Look at that!"

We heaped praise on Keegan, and Dr. Ava urged us to try the exercise ourselves. We clumsily made it through two sets each of web pulls. We were instructed to do a set of twelve pulls on each rear leg, three times a day. It was so rewarding to see her legs move, but it wasn't going to be easy.

Dr. Ava also showed us a "slinky" exercise to do while Keegan was on the exercise ball. You take a paw in each hand and take turns lifting and dropping the rear legs as if you had a slinky in your hands. It simulated a running motion, Dr. Ava explained, reminding her brain how the legs were supposed to work. It was our first introduction to how the connection between the legs and brain was key to recovery.

Next, Dr. Ava's team brought out an electric stimulation device. One of the vet technicians showed us how to use probes along Keegan's neck, spine and paws, spending 30 seconds in each location. She also attached clips to Keegan's ears, sending a smaller dosage of electric current through her body. They told us we could take a unit home with instructions to do the probes and ear clips twice a day. Although the rehab workload was piling up, we were thankful to have all the proper exercises to do with Keegan.

Finally, they took Keegan to the hydrotherapy tank, and we anxiously watched as they prepped the tank. We were a little worried about her reaction. To be honest, Keegan is a big baby. She whines about every little thing, and if her routine gets broken, everyone in the house knows about it. We expected her to freak out. Renea shot me a worried glance as the water began rushing in. Keegan was in this giant glass tank with a doggie life jacket on and a stranger holding her up. All conditions pointed to her having a major meltdown.

When the water hit her front paws, Keegan just looked down with curiosity. As the water rose above her paws, she alternated lifting them up a few times, let out a few whimpers, and then surprisingly went to work. The vet tech hit the treadmill button, and away she went. The person in the treadmill must rest their butt against the back wall of the tank to lean forward, reach down and manually make the dog's back legs walk in step with their front ones. We looked on as Keegan "walked" on the treadmill with the aid of the vet tech. We were two proud parents watching from the sideline as she exercised.

When she was finished, the water drained from the tank, and we sat Keegan in front of a stationary hot air blower. She soaked in the hot air as we toweled her off and waited for Dr. Ava to come in and give us our final instructions. We were leaving with a new plan, a host of different exercises, and extra gear to assist in Keegan's rehab. A new body vest to help carry her around. Stirrups to hook around her back legs to take her for walks and bounce her back legs up and down. And perhaps most importantly, a bag of treats like the ones they had located all across the facility used to reward all the hard-working dogs. All of this was so much better than the generic sling and a pat on the back we received two weeks prior. Although Keegan wasn't fully ready for the intensive rehab, we left Union with a positive outlook on where we were heading.

Keegan's Journal

February 14, 2008

Dear Diary,

Wow!! What a yesterday. I have so much to tell you. Dr. Frick and her staff greeted me with smiles and some of the best cookies that I have ever had. Mom and Dad talked with her for a while. I got an adjustment which felt good! Dr. Ava showed my folks some exercises to help get the feeling back in my legs. Doc also showed them how to use something called Alpha-Stim, which I didn't feel but they said would help. I got in the underwater treadmill, I tried to walk but my back legs would not cooperate, but Doc said that that would all come in time. Mom, Dad and I left with a sack full of goodies for me. Doc gave us a schedule of therapy 3-5 times a day and supplements 3 times a day. So despite not being able to walk, I am going to be a busy girl.

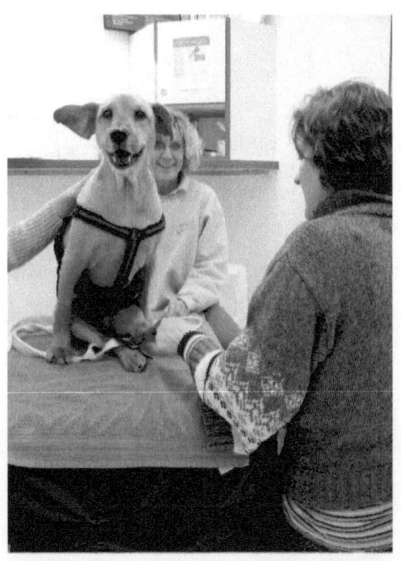

Me with Mommy and Dr. Frick

Chapter 13
Finding a Miracle

Renea and I had been back in Quincy for a little over a year when an event happened that made us both realize just how much we cared for animals. Not just our animals, as we were about to find out, but any and all kinds, and on a deeper level than we could have imagined.

It was a cold December night in 2005, and Renea and I were driving home from the grocery store. We lived on the edge of town and took a less traveled road that skirted the city limits as our route. I was passing through a four-way stop when I saw a small, dark figure on the road about 50 yards ahead.

"What is that?" Renea asked.

"I think it's a raccoon," I answered.

I figured it was some stray critter hunched over a tossed out fast food leftover, but as we neared the figure, the horror quickly materialized. It was a small cat, probably a year old; the rear part of its body ran over by a vehicle. It was trying to crawl to the edge of the road but laboring to move.

I quickly pulled over, and Renea jumped out of the car. She ran over to the cat and scooped it up into her arms. We called our veterinary's emergency number and had a doctor paged. By the time she called back, we were sitting in her clinic parking lot asking if she could come try to save this poor animal. She said she would be there as soon as possible.

We sat in the car as the cat labored to breathe. Blood began trickling out of her nose, and I knew that wasn't a good sign. We sweet talked the cat and massaged her upper body and head, waiting anxiously for what seemed like forever. We told the cat that we would name her "Miracle" if she survived and take her home as part of our family if she could just hold on.

The vet finally arrived, and we rushed into an exam room. We left the cat with her and went back to the lobby to pace. Renea finally lost it and started crying. The vet came out about a half hour later.

"She's in shock," the vet told us. It seems Miracle was female. "I'm having a hard time getting a needle into her vein to sedate her because her blood pressure is so high. I'll keep trying. We'll keep her overnight if she survives and reassess in the morning."

There was nothing else we could do except go home and wait.

Fifteen minutes later, just after arriving home from a very long and eventful trip to the grocery store, the vet called to inform us the cat didn't make it; she was dead.

I walked around with an empty feeling over the next several days. I knew it was because of the whole cat thing but couldn't understand why it bothered me so much. Finally, I sat down and started putting my feelings down on paper. It manifested into a letter to the editor of the local newspaper, meant to warn people to slow down and look out for all the animals who share our roads. The paper published it the following day:

My wife and I were recently driving home on 48th street just north of Columbus Road in Quincy when we saw something odd on the road. At first, it looked like a raccoon leaning over some newfound dinner, but to our horror, as we neared we realized it was a young cat that had been run over, and it was still alive. I quickly pulled over to stop traffic as my wife took off her jacket and scooped the cat (who we later named Miracle in hopes of receiving one) off the road and into her arms. We called our vet's emergency line and sped to her office. For twenty minutes we listened to Miracle's labored breathing, wiped the blood from her mouth and gently stroked her fur, pleading with her to hold on, making the promise of a loving family if she survived. Our vet arrived and much like a scene from E.R., she rushed Miracle into an operating room, and we headed to the waiting area to nervously pace the room.

About 45 minutes later, our vet gave Miracle a 30% chance of survival and told us there was nothing more we could do; they would keep her overnight and hope for the best. Unfortunately, a few minutes after we arrived home, we received the news that Miracle did not pull through and passed away. We asked for a proper burial and spent the rest of the night telling ourselves that although she didn't make it, Miracle was given a dignified death and not one that consisted of lying in the middle of a cold concrete road in the dark where the chance of being hit yet again before finally passing existed.

The next day we returned to our vet's office to pay the bill. A small $200 bill that consisted only of the basic charges and no exorbitant emergency calls is what we paid. When I think back to the 20 short minutes we had with Miracle, the last 20 minutes of her life, I find comfort that she spent them in the arms of two people who truly cared for her and tried their best to will her to stay alive. $200 for 20 minutes...it's the best 10 dollars a minute I'll ever spend.

Please think of this story as you drive to your next destination. Remember that small creatures surround us and cross our roads every day, simply on their way to search for dinner or find a warm place to sleep, and they are no match for the size and speed of an automobile.

Perhaps you can be the miracle for another animal that we didn't receive that night.

Writing the details of that night was therapeutic on many levels. I was able to release the frustration and pain into a purposeful statement. Miracle didn't make it that night, but if one person read that letter and became more aware of animals on the road, then she didn't die in vain. It also helped both Renea and I realize that we did, in fact, do all that we could. We did give her a dignified death, instead of a cold and painful one alone on a dark road.

It also made me realize deep down inside just how much I cared for animals. I had been an animal lover from the start, but now it was turning into something deeper. It was more than an attraction to cute and cuddly creatures. Over the past few years, I had become increasingly frustrated with the way human beings treat each other and the world around them; children and animals, especially. People often asked me why Renea and I didn't have children. I finally had an answer I could give with conviction. "When all the animal shelters are empty," I would say, "we will start thinking about having kids."

Ghandi puts it best when he said, "To my mind, the life of an animal is no less precious than that of a human being. I hold that, the more helpless a creature, the more entitled it is to protection by man from the cruelty of man."

Humans can help themselves. Children, although often mistreated, still have an opportunity to grow up to adulthood and take care of themselves. Animals born into domestication, however, do not have this luxury. For years Quincy had a humane society that operated in a dingy building that was decades old. The shelter in Carbondale, where we adopted Canada and later Jedi, was the same. The story is the same, just insert town name here and you'll likely find underfunded, overcrowded shelters. And while the local shelter had a multi-year fundraiser to build a modern facility, a puppy expo shop opened with expensive breeds of dogs for sale on the busiest street in town. I understand that many people have their heart set on certain breeds of animals, but this feeds into the breeding culture and in the end supports puppy mills. It says a lot about our society when so many people can drive by the animal shelters without batting an eye, on their way to a puppy expo to pay for an animal brought into this world with one sole purpose: for a human to profit financially. So, for years I would say with no qualms, we'll think about having children when all the animal shelters are empty, and the animals have homes.

The following winter would bring about two new additions to the family. In October of 2006, Renea and I came across a Siamese kitten when going to a haunted house in the country. This little kitten ran right to me and jumped up into my arms. I quickly gauged the situation. Here was this tiny little creature, about to face the cold winter months outside, and Siamese cats are not meant to be outdoor cats. I took his eagerness to come to me as a sign, and we took him home. I'm glad we did. After having him checked out by our vet, it turns out he had mites and a severe case of worms. A little TLC from us and medicine from the doctor and he was soon up and running. We named him Keeper because of the split decision I made to keep him.

The eldest member of our cats, Akili, took quite a liking to him. She has always been a loner and the least affectionate of all the cats. We were quite surprised at how the two would pal around the house together side by side, and jokingly dubbed them boyfriend and girlfriend. It was fun to see Akili have a friendship similar to the one shared by Cha and P.J.

In December, Renea's mom found a beautiful calico cat,

estimated to be around six months old, living under a shed behind her house. She lived near one of the busiest intersections in town, and we were amazed the cat made it this long without getting hit. No more animals, we decided, we were at our limit. Four dogs and four cats were enough. We had a big house, for that reason, but had to reach the point and say, "we can't save them all." Renea's mom had a cat at home, Drennan, and said she would try to introduce the calico cat to him. If they got along, she would keep her.

Drennan is a peculiar cat who can go from lovingly rubbing against you to drawing blood by biting you in a second. We all doubted his ability to get along with another cat but gave it a couple of days. In the end, Drennan was just too mean to the cat, and a home had to be found. We agreed to keep the cat at our house while we looked for a home. I had never seen a calico cat with such beautiful markings. It didn't take long for both of us to fall in love with this cute, sweet natured cat. After a few days of searching for a home, with no luck, we decided she would be a perfect addition. We named her Cali. Very original on my part, I know. But she became our little "Cal-Cal," the cat that would announce to everyone she was heading your way by letting out a loud "prrrr" when she jumped. She quickly became everybody's best friend. If one of the other cats is lying on the couch, Cali quickly jumps up with her patented "prrr," and plops down next to them. Everyone except Akili usually allows it. She still only has eyes for Keeper, apparently.

In the end, we weren't able to add Miracle, although we still carry a special place for her in our hearts. We did, however, find two more special cats that have been wonderful additions to the family.

Chapter 14
The Moment We'd Been Waiting For

Keegan's new treatment started right away when we returned home from Union. That evening we did her ball exercises, web pulls, and electric stimulation. She was getting a bit tired of all the exercise, and by the time we switched from the ball to the web pulls, the muzzle had to go back on. We hated to do it, but the exercises had to be done, no way around it. The past twelve hours had been taxing on all of us, so by the time we finished and I took her out for her walk and exercises in her stirrups, which I called her "legs," all three of us were ready for a good night of sleep. We turned her 60s music back on, dimmed the lights, gave her a long goodnight hug, and headed upstairs for bed.

Before bed, however, we needed a small treat. Our trips to St. Louis offered a Dairy Queen conveniently located at the half-way point, which I usually stopped at for a Blizzard. A peanut butter cup Blizzard to be exact. In desperate need of comfort food, I developed the perfect recipe for the homemade Blizzard. A bag of individual peanut butter cups, a tub of ice cream and a blender was all I needed for a soothing end-of-the-evening snack. I'm a bit of a health nut. I try to eat healthy and buy organic when possible. This new development was very out of character, but after all the stress we'd been through the last few weeks, I didn't care. The end-of-day Blizzard would quickly become a new household tradition, to be enjoyed once all of Keegan's evening rehab was finally finished.

I made us both thick, homemade Blizzards with plenty of peanut butter cup chunks in each one. We sat in the living room savoring each spoonful and reflecting on the day. We were both disappointed that Keegan wasn't ready for rehab but thankful that we found Dr. Ava and were anxious to do all the new exercises at home. It was now February 13, just two weeks since Keegan's stroke. I reminded Renea how the rehab process would take months, and we shouldn't lose sight of the long-term goal. We both shared our frustration and agreed to stay patient and keep each other positive. A side lesson I learned from the experience: a lot of problems can be solved over Blizzards. If you've never tried it, I suggest you do. After finishing our Blizzards, I filled the coffee pot, set the timer and finally headed to bed to lay a very weary head down for good.

Six a.m. came with a fog of the eyes and weariness in the bones. After the long seven-hour round-trip to Union, a short night of sleep didn't help either of us. I poured us both cups of coffee and met Renea downstairs, where an equally sleepy Keegan met us with squinty eyes that asked, "Is it morning already?" We had a dry night, which was very exciting; she must have been so tired that even her bladder rested for the night. I put her "legs" on, and we went outside for the morning walk around the driveway, stopping every 20 feet to bounce on the back legs. After expressing the bladder, I took her back inside, where Renea was waiting at the exercise ball. Keegan wasn't a big fan of the ball, and always tried to go straight back to her bed.

"Why do you want to back to bed already?" I would ask her each time, directing her back towards the ball.

She spends all day in the bed; one would think she would enjoy the change of scenery. We created the new exercise routine like an assembly line: First slinky and balance exercises, then she comes off the ball, and Renea does web pulls. By then she's happy to return to the bed, where we do electric stimulus to her back and paws for about 20 minutes. Finally, it was time for her morning medications, before settling in to relax. All in all, the process took about 45 minutes to an hour. It would be time-consuming and tough dragging our tired bodies downstairs every morning, but we were thankful we had so many more new things to try on Keegan. We would have to stay grateful, because this would be our new morning ritual for the foreseeable future.

We would repeat the process two more times each day: Once when we both got home from work around 5 p.m., and again around 9 p.m. before bed. About three hours of rehab a day, every day. By the time the weekend arrived, Renea and I were flat out exhausted. What awaited in the days ahead, however, would give us a renewed sense of energy.

We started our exercises a bit later on the weekends, but thanks to a tricky back I was always up early, so Saturday morning I took Keegan outside to walk and express her. Once back inside, I stopped her on the mats before going back to the bed. I wanted to make sure she was staying clean and sprayed some waterless shampoo on her back legs. When the spray hit her leg, it pulled back on its own. This was the first involuntary movement I'd seen out of Keegs since the stroke more than two weeks earlier. Startled, I just looked at her for a second, and then sprayed the leg again. I got the same result; she pulled her leg up.

"Good girl! Stay there," I told her as if she would get very far on two legs. I ran upstairs and burst into the bedroom.

"Are you up?" I asked Renea.

"What?" she asked in a haze, just coming out of a sleepy slumber.

"Come on, you've got to see something!" I said. She didn't jump right up, so I repeated myself. "Come on, its Keegan, she did something amazing!"

That got Renea moving. She quickly got out of bed and followed me down the stairs. Keegan had listened after all and was in the same place. I sat down next to her and grabbed the shampoo bottle.

"Watch," I said with a smile, and sprayed the leg for a third time, hoping for the same response. Renea watched on in amazement as Keegan pulled her leg up to her rear.

"Oh my god!" she said excitedly.

"I know! I went to wipe her down, and she did that on her own!"

I washed the leg, and we flipped her over to see if we could get the same response out of the other leg. We didn't have the same success with the other side, but we were still ecstatic with any kind of movement. We got her back into bed and rewarded her with lots of goodies and attention. Things started happening quickly after that.

On Sunday I took Keegan outside to express her bladder, and when I lifted my forearm underneath her midsection and lifted, both her back legs lifted a few inches off the ground on their own. She was trying to squat, as she would when she pees on her own. Only instead of squatting towards the ground, she was lifting them in the air. Unlike the shampoo spray the day before, I had to wait for our next bladder expression to show Renea. Later that day, I took her out, and sure enough, she slowly lifted both legs into a squatting position as I expressed her bladder. I don't know if it was a conscious decision or just instinct, but either way, something in her brain was telling her legs to move. What an event!

On Monday, when taking her on an afternoon walk around the driveway, I noticed something else new. When we went on our walks, we stopped every 20 feet to balance on her back legs, holding her up by her support slings, and I would bounce her up and down on her back legs to keep the joints loose. On this afternoon, however, when

I started the bounce, Keegan stayed standing for a second before her legs gave out. It was more like a millisecond, and I thought maybe her joints had locked up. By the next day, however, she was standing for about two seconds before her legs gave out. Unqualified to make an official medical diagnosis, I guessed that we were seeing some strength coming back to the back legs!

Keegan's nickname had been "Thumper" because she wagged her tail so hard it would thump against the floor. If you were standing next to her and she was excited, you might end up with red marks on your leg from her tail whipping into you. It was harrowing to see that once powerful tail now prone, tucked between her legs, but that all changed Monday night. After expressing her outside, I set her legs back down on the ground and noticed something now out of the ordinary…a quick little tail twitch. I made a mental note of it and kept an eye on the tail the next time I took her out to go potty. Sure enough, the next time we were outside the twitch returned, only this time it was more of a quick wag; back and forth just a few inches before settling back down to the tucked position. It appeared she was quite happy with her bathroom trips and was now showing me with a tail wag!

>Tuesday, February 19, 2008
>Dr. Ava,
>
>Just wanted to send you a progress report on Keegan. She seems to be getting stronger in the back legs. When we take her for walks and stop every 20 feet, sometimes she can support herself for a few seconds before falling into a sitting position.
>
>We're starting to get a little resistance when we do the slinky exercises. Also, when cleaning her up this weekend, I sprayed some waterless shampoo spray on her legs, to

which she pulled her leg up to her side without any assistance from us. I later sprayed some water on them (to demonstrate to Renea) and the leg pulled up again on its own.

When we take her out to potty, she lifts both legs as if she would normally do when squatting. We didn't have any of that the first two weeks. She is now finishing her bathroom breaks with a tail wag – we're seeing a lot more movement in her tail, it's not just tucked in-between her legs anymore.

Lastly – she's trying awful hard to lift up her hindquarters. No power in the legs yet, but her rear torso area seems to be getting stronger. Hope all of these are positive signs!

Travis

Wednesday, February 20, 2008
Wow!!!!!!! This is wonderful!!!!!!! Congratulations!!!!!!!
We need to schedule her Sunday return. Would 3 PM work for you?

Dr. Ava

We spent the rest of the week watching Keegan improve. Her tail wag seemed to grow each day. By Friday she could wag her tail for about five seconds after going to the bathroom and occasionally when on the exercise ball. We were excited to report all the good news to Dr. Ava and get her started on the underwater treadmill. By the time Sunday came, however, I wasn't quite ready to see her go.

I had spent more time with Keegan in the past two weeks than I probably had in the previous two months. The downside to rescuing animals is you get a lot of paws pulling you in different directions. It's hard to give everyone the attention they rightfully deserve. Outside of our walks in the morning, we didn't really have any quality one-on-one time with the dogs. Renea and I knew we were probably beyond our limit. We wanted them to all get the attention they deserved and told ourselves that in the future we would try to limit the number of animals we owned. For the time being we had to make it work with the clan that we had. With all the extra time spent together in the past few weeks, I was developing quite a bond with Keegan. As much as Renea and I were both looking forward to having a break from all the work for a few days, it was hard knowing she was going to be gone again.

The upcoming rehab meant additional bills, so our search for a new home continued. Unfortunately, we weren't getting very far. I understand that in the process of downsizing, you have to be willing to give up certain amenities. What we were finding, however, was less than desirable. We looked at a ranch home in a decent albeit cramped neighborhood. The house had an add-on, so we were excited at the prospect of retaining much of the badly needed space our current home offered. Once inside, however, the excitement quickly waned. The entire house had been splashed with a sterile coat of white, and the ceiling consisted of large panels, many of which were sagging.

"What's with the ceiling?" I asked the realtor, having never seen such a style in a home before.

"Well, that's called cheap, Travis," she said.

I appreciated her frankness, but we high-tailed it out of the home nonetheless. Our search took us all over Quincy, but every house was too small, too expensive, too ugly, or in a crummy part of town. It seemed every single listing had some check mark against it. Then we came across a remodeled two-story home with promise. For what we needed, it had everything; lots of space inside, a fenced in backyard, and it was all remodeled, from the flooring to the paint. The skeptic in me thought that judging from the affordable list price, this house this was too good to be true. The chance of finding everything we needed in a good looking home for thousands less than ours was slim to none, I was beginning to think, and didn't want to get myself excited about this house until we knew all the facts.

Buying a home is a tricky proposition. There are all sorts of underlying issues, some that come up during the home buying process, others that you might not find out about until long after you've purchased the home. Some detective work is needed, where you can feel comfortable that you have all the facts before committing to such a large financial obligation. The facts on this attractive little number were this: the seller of the home was a local home inspector. By law, they aren't allowed to inspect a house they are selling, so someone else did the inspection. I was curious to see said inspection, and we made a follow-up appointment to go through the house with my father-in-law, Gerald. He was quite the handyman and was currently gutting and remodeling a house from the ground up. We trusted his word over the word of an unknown home inspector every day of the week and twice on Sunday.

The next few days were emotional for both of us as we waited for the follow-up walkthrough in the house. We would go from being excited about the new home, which featured an open floor plan and hardwood floors in the kitchen and dining room, to being depressed about leaving the home we'd lived in for nearly three years. Back and forth we would go until finally, the day arrived to inspect the potential new home thoroughly.

Unfortunately, my initial skepticism of the house was warranted. Gerald went through the house pointing out everything wrong with it. As it turned out, the guy selling it flipped homes and did a shoddy job at that. While we were sad to have missed out on what could have been a perfect fit for us, we were lucky to dodge a bullet in buying a money pit. It was back to the drawing board for the house search. But time was of the essence with new rehabilitation expenses rapidly approaching.

The typical scene before starting morning rehab

Keegan's Journal

February 17, 2008

Dear Diary,

I moved my back legs today!!! Mom and Dad tried to spray me with some shampoo and I showed them that I did not like it. I kicked at them with my back legs!!!!! I know that I am getting stronger, Mom and Dad take me on walks and I can hold my own weight for a few seconds now. It makes us all smile!!!!!! Some of the exercises that Mom and Dad do are getting old, so I show them that I don't like it by resisting. One small twitch for Keegan, one giant twitch for dog-kind, as Dad says!!!

Chapter 15
What's Going on Here?

In April of 2007 tragedy hit our family and it hit us hard. I'd been keeping an eye on Cha for over a week, noticing he was not quite himself. Of all our animals, he was the one most commonly taken to the vet for various ailments. I assumed this was just another ailment. I was wrong.

The initial diagnosis by our vet was a virus of some sort, and our doctor sent us home on a Friday with antibiotics. Sunday night I found Cha in our bedroom closet with a clear fluid coming out of his mouth. I paged our vet, and when he called I explained Cha's symptoms. He said they couldn't do anything overnight and told us to bring him in first thing in the morning. After they got another look at him, they found that his abdominal cavity had filled up with fluid. They ran all sorts of tests and wanted to keep him for a few days. His condition worsened, and they narrowed it down to two things, fatty liver disease or a rare feline disease known as FIP. According to our vet, most cats are exposed to FIP when they are young but develop immunity to it. Some adult cats with inadequate immune systems can be susceptible to it. There currently is no cure for FIP. There was nothing we could do for Cha except wait for the test results.

Meanwhile, Bud had gone downhill in the past year. Now 17 years old, he had developed a nasty cough because his lungs were filling up with fluid. The situation was unrelated to Cha; it was just a condition of old age. Medication helped, but the poor little guy still hacked an awful lot. Bud and Jedi were the two male dogs in the house, and they did not get along. We did our best to cohabitate them, but they never could get it together. Thankfully we had space at our new home in Quincy to keep them separate, and because it was hard for Bud to get up and down the stairs, the basement was semi-adopted as Bud's Castle. He had his own little bed and feeding station down there and enjoyed the peace and quiet. We would bring Bud upstairs in the evening and Jedi would retire to our bedroom.

Wednesday morning of that week, I called from the basement to let all the dogs out. Keegan and Canada came running down, but no Bud. He was very hard of hearing on top of everything else, so this was no surprise. I went upstairs, calling his name again. I knew right where to find him; his favorite sleeping spot was next to the couch near *my* favorite spot. Sure enough, there he was in his usual place. I called from the top of the stairs once again, but he didn't move. My stomach dropped as I slowly walked over to him. It only took a moment to realize what had happened. My old faithful friend had passed away in his sleep.

I dropped to my knees and started bawling. I had lost a few pets as a child, but never as an adult and never one this close to my heart. Every cell in my body ached as I pressed my head against his body. His body was cold and stiff. His tongue hung out of the side of his mouth. Seeing him up close just made me cry harder, something I didn't think possible. I curled up on the floor next to him for about five minutes, just crying and talking to him. Seventeen years is a long time, and to have a dog as loyal, loving and faithful as Bud is something I wish everyone could experience once in their life. I got to experience it for nearly two decades. I was lucky.

I picked myself up off the floor and called Renea at work. She was already teetering on the emotional edge waiting to hear about Cha, so she took the rest of the day off. She came home and helped me get Bud wrapped up in a blanket to take to the vet. I paced for several minutes before we left, not ready to have Bud leave the house for the last time. Finally, we walked out the back door with Bud in my arms. I gently placed him in the back of the SUV and Renea drove us to the veterinary office. They led us into an exam room, and I laid him down on the table, uncovering his head. I sat with him for a few minutes, thanking him one last time for nearly 20 years of loyalty and friendship. Then the doctor came in, and we discussed what to do with his body. I wanted to have him cremated. At the time I thought I would spread his ashes at my Grandmother's land in nearby Lima, Ill. Bud's death took the wind out of our sails. Friday morning, a phone call from our vet took the air out of our lungs. Cha slipped away quietly early Friday morning.

In the end, the FIP had been too much for him to fight. He put up a valiant effort, but ultimately nature won out. Two days earlier, I lost the most loyal animal I'd ever known. Now I'd lost the sweetest, most amazing creature I ever came across. I dreadfully made the call to Renea at work, and she burst into tears at the news. Even though we both knew it was inevitable, we still weren't prepared. I was still in an emotional haze from losing Bud two days prior. Now it was Renea's turn to lose it.

We met outside the vet's office, and I held Renea as she cried and cried. I was either out of tears or too stunned at this point to cry anymore. "Out of tears," right? I'm sure there are tons of songs written about that. Now I understood why. After about five minutes sitting outside in the car, we went inside. They led us to the same exam room, where we waited for the doctor to bring in Cha. Renea lost it all over again when they brought our little white bundle into the room. I sat in a chair against the wall with my head down in my hands. Renea went to say goodbye to Cha, now on the exam table. The day before when I was in to see Cha, he seemed to have a bit more energy and the last thing he did was stand up against my chest and rub his nose against mine, something he did so many times before.

"There's my little Cha!" I said to him even though I knew he couldn't hear.

Even though he never could hear us, we found a way to communicate more with him than any other of our animals. It was a weird and amazing connection we shared with him. I wanted to keep that as my last memory of him. Renea told him how sorry she was and how much we would miss him. After what seemed like hours, the doctor came back in to once again ask us about what to do with his body.

"What's going on here?" Renea asked. "We've lost two of our pets in three days, should we be worried?"

It was a valid question, but fortunately (or unfortunately, depending on how you look at it) it was just a matter of very bad timing that we lost two of our beloved pets in such a short span.

Bud's death was hard, but it was not a complete shock, and he went exactly how I'd hope he would, peacefully in his sleep. Cha, on the other hand, was an entirely different story. He was taken from us after only five short years. I told myself he lived three times the life of any normal cat; therefore, he wasn't really shortchanged. It's true; he did live life more than any other cat. Most cats will lie around all day and generally have a lackadaisical approach to humans. Once Cha knew you were home, he couldn't get close enough to you. He would fall asleep on the backrest of the couch resting against your head, or push up right against your face, or under the blanket, anywhere or anything to get close. He once found a way to pry open one of the heat vent covers and go exploring through the ventilation shafts in our house.

We spent days trying to get the soot out of his coat. He climbed up into the drop ceiling in our basement by way of sneaking into the laundry room, climbing up on top of the stackable washer and dryer, and hopping up into the ceiling. He knocked a screen out of an upstairs bedroom and hopped down from the second floor to investigate the neighborhood. Thankfully our neighbor found him. If there was trouble to find, he would find it. More importantly, if there was love to give, he was first in line to give it. I do not exaggerate when I attempt to describe what a fantastic creature he was.

For days I thought I would catch a glimpse of Cha in the corner of my eye, only to remember he was gone. He shed everywhere, and for months we came across "Cha hair" which would just make us start crying again. We think back now to that terrible week when we lost two members of our family and like to think that Bud sensed that Cha would be gone soon and wanted to be there to meet him in pet heaven. I don't know much about pet heaven, but I certainly hope one exists. The spirit of an animal is so beautiful and pure, and their actions speak for themselves.

Bud and Cha

Chapter 16
Round One in the Books

Sunday afternoon we loaded all of Keegan's things into the back of the SUV and headed back to Union for the second time. This time we hoped Keegan would be sticking around for some intensive therapy that we couldn't offer her at home. We got about halfway there when the downpour began. Of course it did. The winding roads through the hills of Missouri weren't very friendly in dry weather, never mind slick roads. *Three for three*, I thought. First, it was fog, then sleet, now rain to complete the trifecta. I patiently weaved through the hills as Renea and I discussed what we were going to do with the next few days with no rehab, no manual expressing, and no electrical probing to do.

"Rest," I said, offering my best guess. "And spend some time with our other animals."

Having survived the rain, we arrived at Dr. Ava's office and again got out and stretched before getting Keegan out of the truck. I took Keegan for a walk with her "legs" around the complex before going in. Dr. Ava met us outside the front door. I was quick to show off her progress.

"We're standing for about five seconds!" I said, showing off Keegan's new skill. While standing, she began wagging her tail.

"This is great progress," Dr. Ava said. "Usually you don't see this before ten days of rehab. Once it starts, it all happens fast."

That was exciting news, and it meant she was ready for the intense stuff with the good Dr. Ava! Renea took Keegan inside and I went back to the truck to get Keegan's things.

Giant doggie bed, check. Bag of large chewies, check. A Smaller bag of treats, check. Peanut butter filled Kong, check. Vitamins and supplements, check. Electric probe unit, check. Giant chicken flavored bone toy that we couldn't get her to play with, check. Keegan was turning into quite the high maintenance lady! Three loads later, Keegan was all settled in her large kennel with a window view, and Renea and I were ready to turn around and head back to Quincy. We thanked Dr. Ava and made arrangements to pick her up Thursday evening. With that, we were again on our way home. Before we made it to the highway, however, we saw an Arby's restaurant close to the doctor's office. One thing about going through stressful times is you quit caring about other things, like how you'll look in a swimsuit the following summer. We attacked the "five for five" menu and pigged out on roast beef sandwiches, jamocha milkshakes, cherry turnovers, curly fries and more. Just about all the greasy food our stomachs could handle. Five minutes after hitting the highway, we were both agreeing with our stomachs that maybe the Arby's wasn't such a good idea. We gutted it out and made it home in one piece, perhaps a few pounds heavier.

Renea and I spent the next week continuing our house search. After striking out on the earlier house and not coming across anything new on the market in our price range, we started weighing all our options. We discussed our situation with my folks, who urged us to try to keep the house and look into refinancing our current mortgage. It was an idea we had kicked around but looked at it as robbing Peter to pay Paul in a sense, because we'd simply be transferring debt, not eliminating it. We continued our house search but kept the refinancing idea in the back of our minds.

Despite being broke, Renea and I splurged and went out to dinner on Wednesday night. Dinner and drinks were just what the doctor ordered on our last night of freedom, so to speak, before Keegan returned home. Over drinks, we talked more about the house situation, discussed how sweet Keegan was being through the entire ordeal, and how good our other animals had been despite the lack of attention. It was a nice end to a relaxing couple of days.

Thursday we made the trek to Union, but this time I had finally had it with the winding two-lane highways and back roads. I mapped us out a new route that took us towards St. Louis and away from Union but kept us on a four-lane interstate the entire trip. In the end, the trip took the same amount of time but came with much less frustration by leaving behind winding roads and slow trucks on two-lane roads. I was extremely pleased with my newfound route. A small victory. I was taking any that I could get.

The four-day break we had from the duties of caring for Keegan was restful, but we were anxious to bring her home. For the past month, every day began with waking up a sleepy Keegan, taking her outside to be manually expressed, and getting her day started with a session of electric probing. Not having her around for the past four days was a nice break physically but a challenge emotionally.

We walked into the front door of the complex and one of Dr. Ava's assistants, Quintana, greeted us with a smile.

"You're going to be so excited!" she said. "We just started kicking our back legs in the last 24 hours!" Seeing is believing, I thought, not wanting to get my hopes up.

She took us back to the kennel area and I quickly climbed into the kennel to greet Keegan. She was incredibly happy to see us and hobbled over to crash into me. After loving her up for a minute, I was eager to see her progress. We got her legs on and Quintana led her outside.

I have to admit; we were both disappointed. Quintana's description of Keegan kicking her legs was more of a small, occasional twitch as she was led around in her sling. Renea was visibly disappointed. I told myself they've been doing this a long time, so if she was excited about this progress, it must be good.

The cost for four days of rehab added up to around $800. At least this time we were prepared for the financial impact (even if we weren't sure how we'd pay for it). We weighed all of this beforehand and decided that we'd already spent nearly $4,000 just to find out what was wrong with Keegan. We wouldn't be doing her justice by not spending at least that much to try to get her well.

We met with Dr. Ava and talked about new exercises and vitamins for Keegan and scheduled to bring her back in ten days for another four-day rehab stint. Overall, Dr. Ava said she was pleased with what she saw from Keegan and told us we should expect continued improvement. I had to ask the obvious question.

"After spending time with her, do you think she'll walk again?" I asked.

"She's certainly improving," Dr. Ava told us. "If we continue the rehab here and at home, I think she'll make it." That's what we needed to hear.

I loaded up Keegan's bed and supplies while Renea paid the bill. Finally, we loaded Keegan back into the truck, and shortly after 8 p.m. we began the three-hour trip back to Quincy. By the time we arrived home, got Keegan inside and situated, and our other dogs outside and back in, it was midnight. 6:15 a.m. rehab with Keegan was right around the corner. Much like after our last trip to Union, Renea and I collapsed into bed at the end of the day, physically and emotionally exhausted, but with one round of intensive rehab in the books.

Keegan's Journal

February 24, 2008

Dear Diary,

We went to Dr. Ava again, this time I got to stay with them for a while to get more therapy. I am not scared at all because all the staff here is great. Quintana is the one that gets to work with me and she is very good and gentle. I will miss Mom and Dad, but I will work hard just for them!!!! My routine here is pretty rigorous. I have to do the underwater treadmill two times a day, Quin is in with me moving my back legs for me. She really enjoys working with me. I also get the Alpha-Stim therapy and exercises two times a day. With all the supplements and caring for me. I see why all the animals are happy to come here.

Preparing for underwater treadmill therapy

Chapter 17
The Breakthrough

On a crisp, sunny Saturday afternoon we got the breakthrough we desperately needed to keep us going. We strapped Keegan into her wheelchair and took her for an early afternoon stroll through the neighborhood. She still hadn't figured out all the nuances of this new metal contraption attached to the lower half of her body, but she was trying. Once you got her going, she would do ok, but Renea would have to give her a little push from behind to get her moving, and I would lead her with the leash. About a half a block into our walk, we noticed something...her back legs began to kick. I'm not talking about the tiny little kicks we first saw when Quintana walked her around the complex in Union; these were full-fledged steps! In the chair, Keegan's back legs are strapped into stirrups to keep them from dragging along the ground. Instead of hanging lifeless in the stirrups as they had been, they were coming to life.

You could see the thought process from brain to paw was a slow one. About every three steps she took with her front legs, you would get one kick out of one of the back legs. Another three steps and the other rear leg would kick. It was incredible to watch. We were practically skipping with joy as we trotted along with Keegan, doing her continuous three-step and kick routine. It wasn't walking, but it solidified what Dr. Ava told us, and made all the hours of rehab and probing we'd done worthwhile.

We finished the walk and got Keegan back in her basement "den," as Renea had started calling it. We praised her with love and treats for her amazing feat. Just weeks ago, in that very bed, we barely got a muscle twitch in her rear legs. Now she was kicking on her own. And she wasn't about to stop. Later that afternoon when I put her in her sling and took her out, she continued her kicking every couple steps as we walked through the yard. If this was helped along by the four-day rehab stint, I couldn't wait to see what another four days would do.

The only problem with that was another trip to Union meant another hefty bill, and we were tapped out. We needed to come to a decision on what we were going to do about our home, and soon. Renea and I continued to go back and forth on what to do about the decision to downsize or refinance. The advantage to selling was huge; we could wipe out a significant amount of our debt in one move. The benefits to refinancing our current home were many smaller factors; we loved our home and wanted to stay in it, we wouldn't have the added burden of trying to sell the house quick and moving was never cheap. It wasn't until we started debating how we would go about selling the house that some clarity came to us.

We still couldn't decide which was best, a bridge loan or making an offer with a contingency to sell. Because of our current situation, I was in favor of the bridge loan. Our setup had Keegan in the basement, two other dogs upstairs, and five cats occupying one of the upstairs bedrooms with their "cat room," complete with a kitty door. To sell the house quick, we would have to do something with Keegan every time someone wanted a showing, replace the door to the cat room, kennel the dogs every day, and keep the house spotless. We barely had enough time to stop and catch our breath as it was, and I didn't see how doing all of this would be a reality.

Renea felt a bridge loan was too big of a risk, and instead thought we should make an offer on a house with the contingency to sell ours, and then try to sell ours as fast as possible. With all the animals still in the house and nowhere to go with Keegan, I disagreed with the strategy. We were at an impasse, and honestly, neither option was very practical. As enticing as eliminating such a huge chunk of debt was, the scale of what to do started to tip in favor of refinancing. Renea made an appointment to meet with a loan officer at our bank to discuss our options and possibly get the ball rolling. Meanwhile, Keegan's rehab rolled on. The following Sunday, after ten days back at home, we made the familiar trip to Missouri for her second extended rehab stint. We decided that financially this would have to be her final trip for a while. We just couldn't afford to take her down for extended stays every ten days. We made the seven-hour round-trip for the third time that month and prayed that she would make great strides again.

During the following four-day break, Renea and I mapped out a strategy for getting out of the financial crisis we were in through refinancing our home. While it didn't eliminate the debt, it certainly would help make things more manageable. We added up all the figures, and with a 100% refinance we would be able to wipe out most of our credit card debt. We were still a few thousand short of starting fresh when my mother said she and my step-father, Andy, wanted to talk with us before we made a decision. When we met, they listened to our options and made a generous proposal. They wanted us to be able to stay in our current home, so they offered us a low-interest loan to wipe out the remaining credit card debt not covered by our refinance loan. So that was that. Thanks to the generosity of my folks and a bank willing to refinance 100% of the value of our house, we were finally able to pay off the high-interest credit card debt that was weighing on us like an anvil. It was such a generous offer by two people that, ironically, didn't have a single pet. But they knew how much our pets and home meant to us and came through in a great time of need.

It was a blessing finally knowing that we would be staying in the home we had made so many improvements to and loved so much. Renea and I spent an evening calling all our credit card companies and canceling all but one of our accounts. Surprisingly, this was no easy task. Credit card company employees must make commission based on how long they keep customers on the phone, because simple calls were turning into marathons. I would be on one phone turning down offer after offer to stay with the company; meanwhile, Renea was on her phone attempting to get a live representative on the line. One person even became combative when I tried to cancel our account as if I was hurling personal insults at her. *We're just trying to pay you the money we owe you!* Finally, after two hours, we succeeded in canceling all but one emergency credit card and tucked it away for just that, an emergency. Thursday's trip to Union was a little more relaxed with our debt problems behind us and the uncertainty of where we would be living finally resolved.

Keegan's Journal

March 1, 2008

Dear Diary,

I'm starting to kick my back legs! I was on a walk in my wheelchair, telling my back legs to work along with my front ones when it happened. My legs, held up in stirrups, would kick about every third step. The process of getting the message from my brain to my back legs is a slow one but it is starting to happen! My parents just did a silly dance in the middle of the street. The neighbors probably now think we're all crazy.

Chapter 18
"I Didn't Think She'd Ever Walk Again"

According to the employees in Dr. Ava's office, it was another productive four days of therapy for Keegan. She was standing a lot longer and making significant progress on the underwater treadmill. Dr. Ava changed some of her supplements and sent us home with a few new instructions. Now that Keegs was starting to support herself, we needed to concentrate on her balancing skills. What good is a dog that can stand if it can't balance, right? The balance exercise consisted of side to side motions while balancing Keegan on the ball to support her when she starts to sway left or right. We were to add that to our first set of rehab exercises and continue as instructed. We loaded Keegan back into the truck and headed back home. I was excited to tell Keegan that she wouldn't be moving; I don't think she cared.

That weekend, I noticed two things that concerned me. Keegan had developed a few spots on her back legs where the fur was turning a darker shade of brown. The areas didn't seem to be sensitive to the touch, but anything out of the ordinary worried me. The other thing I was keeping an eye on was a small pouch that had been developing between her rear legs on her buttocks. There was nothing out of the ordinary on her fur or skin; it was more of a bulge that seemed to be on the inside. At the time it wasn't large enough to warrant any care, but by the following weekend, it was large enough to alarm me. I thought a checkup with our Quincy vet, Dr. Reich, was overdue anyway, and realized that he hadn't seen her since her initial stroke nearly two months ago. On Monday morning I called and made an appointment for a routine checkup. I was also anxious to show him and all the wonderful assistants at the clinic how well Keegan was doing.

Later that week I strapped Keegan into her legs and we headed to the veterinary office. As soon as we got inside, the receptionist's face lit up, remembering Keegan from her initial stay.

"We're doing great!" I said, and as if taking that as a cue, Keegan began peeing in the lobby. "OK, maybe not!" I said sheepishly and awkwardly tried to get Keegan outside. Before I could, she started to poop.

"That's the Keegan I know and love," I said to her once outside. She had a habit of losing what little control of her bladder and bowels she had when excited, and apparently being back in the vet's office did just that to her.

Once she was fully relieved (I hoped) we headed back inside, where two of the vet technicians were there to greet Keegan. She was happy to oblige, and her tail started wagging. I thought this was a wonderful opportunity for her to show off her accomplishments. Whenever my spirits were down during Keegan's rehab, I would stop myself and think of how hard this all was on her. That would always snap me back into a clearer perspective. She was trying to come back from paralysis, and her improvement thus far was incredible. I was one proud dog owner watching the vet techs love Keegan up, and Keegan enjoying every second of it.

That all ended once we made it into the exam room. The scared and whiny Keegan returned. Dr. Reich came in, and it took both of us and the vet assistant to keep her steady while the hum of a motor kicked on, raising the automatic exam table to a normal height. While trying to calm Keegan down, I gave Dr. Reich and update on her progress. He spent a good deal of time doing the routine examination, followed by a closer look at the spots on her leg and the bulge near her buttocks. He diagnosed the spots as some sort of change in the skin where no sore or infection ever developed. He pointed out where the spots, two on each leg, were the pressure points where most of her weight falls on when lying on her side. Because she slept on a top-notch orthopedic bed and we had been diligent in turning her over, they never developed into bedsores. He assessed that they were nothing out of the ordinary, and there was no need to worry.

The bulge was sagging muscles. There is a wall of muscles in between both rear legs, and as the rear leg muscles atrophied, so did that wall, causing the bulge. Again, nothing to worry about, he told us.

"She's had a lot of positive progress," he told us. "You should see those muscles tighten back up as her back legs get stronger."

I was relieved to find out that both issues were nothing to worry about. After Keegan's injury and Cha's death, I'd begun to expect the worst and hope for the best. The last thing Dr. Reich did was pull out a needle to test Keegan's deep pain response. When the initial stroke happened, she felt nothing just past her front shoulder blades. He started at the base of her tail and didn't have to poke very far before getting a response. He was amazed at how much feeling had returned in two months.

"I have to be honest," he turned and said to me. "I didn't want to say anything when you and Renea first brought her in, but I didn't think she would ever walk again." Tears began welling up in his eyes. "This is a true testament that good things do still happen. You guys took a huge leap of faith and have been just wonderful for her."

It's not every day you bring your vet to tears. I was so proud of Keegan at that moment. I had my suspicions about our doctors' true feelings when the neurologist told us not to expect a good prognosis, but no one ever came out and said it. Now Dr. Reich was confirming that he initially thought Keegan would be paralyzed for life. Keegan was beating the odds. Somebody forgot to tell her that her back legs didn't work, and she was bound and determined to get moving again.

As winter slowly turned into spring that April, our trips outside became more than just bathroom breaks, but mini-rehab sessions. I would simulate walking outside in her slings by bouncing up and down as we walked, allowing her to take "steps" in the air, then dropping her feet back to the ground. Keegan also went for her first official walk without her wheelchair. Instead of the chair, I used the sling to help support her. We made it about two blocks before my arms tired out from holding the sling up and we headed back. We were certainly taking baby steps towards normalcy, but Keegan taking any type of step, both real and metaphorically, was huge for all of us. The light at the end of the tunnel we only *hoped* was there months ago was starting to appear. Our sweet girl was learning how to walk again.

Later that week, I came home from work to an incredible sight; Keegan was standing on her bed eating from her food bowl. Up until now she would pull herself up to the fireplace ledge and eat sitting down. As of late, she was trying to stand, only to have her legs give out on her.

"Keegan, look at you!" I exclaimed.

I rushed to the other side of the room and grabbed the camera, thinking she was going to be back on her butt any second. She continued, standing and eating as I snapped away taking photos. Keegan was probably wondering why I was making such a fuss over her merely eating her dinner. It was so much more; it was another step in the long road of her recovery, and a piece of normalcy returning to her life.

Renea and I agreed that after this latest breakthrough, it would be good to start bringing Keegan upstairs for a few hours a night. We had kept her free from bedsores and infections during the first few months, and I thought with her beginning to get back on her feet, she could take the trek up and down the stairs. I strapped her legs on, and Keegan ventured back up the stairs for the first time in nearly three months. We put Jedi up in our bedroom, fearing his rambunctious style wouldn't mesh well with Keegan, who was still technically a down dog. Keegan seemed happy to be back upstairs with all her brothers and sisters. Canada seemed equally happy to have her back.

With Keegan making such big strides in her rehab, we decided to step it up a notch and start walking her on our home treadmill. So far, the only real walking she had done was on the underwater treadmill at Dr. Ava's facility in Union. We had a regular treadmill in our basement and decided to put it to good use. Renea stood above Keegan, holding her harness to help support her weight, while I crouched at the base of the machine to guide her back legs. Renea turned the treadmill on low, and Keegan was not happy about it. She locked her front legs up to foil any rehab plans we had for the day. We fought back, telling her she was going to do this whether she liked it or not. After a few stop-and-go tries, we finally got her going.

With our help, Keegan walked on the treadmill for about three minutes before we had to take a break. Renea was supporting most of Keegan's weight by holding her up by her harness, and one can only hold up 50 pounds or so for a short time. My ankles were screaming anyway, so I was happy to stop. Crouched down trying to keep her back feet moving in a smooth motion, I thought either of my Achilles tendons could burst at any moment. We stopped for a few minutes, praising Keegan and giving her treats. After resting, we started the treadmill again and went for another three or four minutes. With our help, Keegan was taking real steps on her own. They were sloppy and plodding, but her brain and back legs were making a connection, and that was more important than style points.

We began doing the home treadmill therapy sessions twice a day. In a little more than three months, Keegan had graduated from range of motion exercises and "twinkle-toes," garnering barely more than a small muscle twitch, to taking steps on a treadmill. It was quite an accomplishment, and we were sure to let her know every day with lots of love and treats. With her routine rehab exercises now coupled with frequent trips upstairs and prolonged "walks" outside, she was pretty tuckered out by the end of each day. Renea and I, on the other hand, were finally beginning to feel the fog lift. Thanks to my parents' help and refinancing our home, our debt was no longer hanging over our heads. Keegan was showing amazing improvement, which made all the hard work we'd put in worth it. Things were looking up.

Keegan's Journal

March 8, 2008

Dear Diary,

Rehab is pretty intense since I have been home. I rest on an exercise ball and my parents do "slinkys" with my back legs to simulate a stair stepper. Then it's on to toe pinches, where they pull the webbing in-between my toes until my leg pulls back. After some range of motion exercises, I get the Alpha-Stim therapy. That's where my nerve endings from my brain to the parts of my body that don't work so well are remapped using tiny electrical impulses. I don't feel any pain when they do my therapy. I really like the ear clip part. I feel really relaxed after that is done and normally take a nap. It's all working and I keep kicking my back legs on my walks!

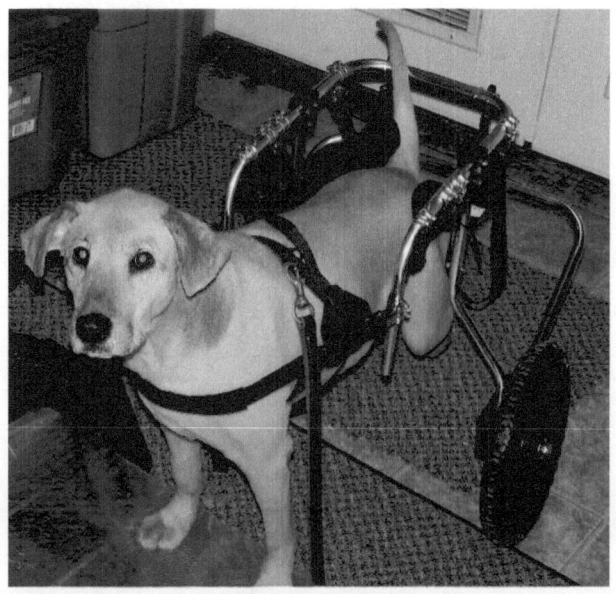

Ready to roll!

Chapter 19
Everything Old is New Again

By the end of April, Keegan was taking steps in her sling without the aid of me lifting her up off the ground. She was even trying to walk around the living room when we had her upstairs, but her little legs just weren't strong enough to hold her weight up yet. We hit a wall of sorts with her rehab and decided one more trip to Dr. Ava would serve her well. Over the past few months, I'd looked forward to the four-day rest that came with Keegan's stay in Union. This time, it was a different story. We'd made such great strides, and the rehab was now less of a physical strain on both of us. I'd taken to jumping into her "den" and just lying on the dog beds with her, talking aimlessly about whatever came to mind. She had become a pretty good listener over the past few months. I love all of our animals and share a bond with them all, but this new connection I had made with Keegan was now something different, something stronger. Renea noticed it as well, saying Keegan didn't know what to do when I was out of the room. If I left the upstairs, she would make her way to the top of the steps and whine until I came back.

As the annual Thursday trip arrived, it seemed like I was finally going to get some cooperation from Mother Nature, as I had sunny skies the entire way there. Spring was finally here, which meant the sun was just setting when I arrived in Union. The round-trip excursions over the past few months were not easy with cold weather, harsh driving conditions, and nightfall coming just as we would leave Quincy.

The changing seasons made the trip more bearable, and it was nice to load Keegan up for the trip home Sunday evening in daylight. I could tell her strength was beginning to return to her back legs because she kept trying to stand the entire way back to Quincy. I arrived home around 10:30 p.m. and set about the familiar task of unloading her bed and all her goodies from the truck and getting the basement situated. I was anxious to see her progress, so after she ate dinner I moved some of the crates surrounding her beds so she could try to walk around in the basement. The last few days proved to be fruitful, as she mastered yet another move: the pivot.

Keegan had built up enough strength to stand and could take steps on her own, but up to this point she was still wobbly and couldn't put it all together. This time her progress allowed her to change direction without falling over. Anytime she would try to turn her body while standing up, she would fall over onto her butt or side. Now she could turn from one direction to another and keep her balance by shifting her back legs. Slowly but surely, she was getting there!

The month of May was full of milestones. The first was Keegan spending the night upstairs for the first time since January. As she began to recover some of her abilities, she also developed a sense of restlessness. Spending the day on a plush doggie bed when you're paralyzed is one thing; when your capacity to walk comes back, it's a different story. We decided to open up her area to include more of the basement floor and not just the two beds. This way if she wanted to try and walk, she could do it on a firm floor and not the soft bedding. I was trying to keep life as exciting as I could for her, so I thought alternating nights upstairs and down would help. There was a small problem with this. Keegan was able to hold her bladder downstairs ok, where she was just a few feet from the door in the morning. After spending the night upstairs, we had to carry her down the stairs with the aid of her harness, which put pressure directly on her bladder. That, of course, equaled pee.

Keegan also tended to pee when she got excited. She was doing her best to hold her bladder, but if she got too excited, all that went out the window. Well, on the floor, to be accurate. It was as if when she was excited her brain would forget to tell her bladder to stay shut, and out it came. When I would come out of the bedroom in the morning, she was either super excited to see me or excited to be going outside, and nature's floodgates would open. It wasn't a lot, not nearly as much as when she I manually expressed her, but enough to warrant getting out the carpet cleaner. We had a secret weapon, though.

Because Jedi was never formally potty-trained as a pup, we were never able to fully train him as an inside dog. After first moving to Quincy, we found out the hard way that Jedi was marking certain spots of the house when we were gone. We finally realized this when the power went out in one section of the house. We called an electrician when we couldn't figure it out ourselves. After investigating, he finally diagnosed the problem: a soggy electrical socket.

"You've got some moisture in one of the outlets on this wall," the electrician told me. "Quite a bit, actually, it's as if someone spilled something in it." I did my best to keep a straight face.

"Hmmm," I feigned curiosity.

But I'd already put it together. Jedi peed in the electrical wall socket, shorting out a section of the house. I didn't have the heart to tell the electrician he was holding a pee-soaked outlet in his hand.

"Now that sure is odd." I said, completing the facade.

How Jedi didn't electrocute himself, I'll never know. He probably got quite a jolt; I can garner that much for sure. He is oblivious to the rest of the world at times, and this was apparently one of them.

We solved the problem by purchasing a cloth dog diaper for him. It wasn't that he couldn't hold it; he just didn't know any better. At this point in his life, we couldn't unlearn the habit of him peeing whenever he had to, so we did the next best thing and wrapped him up! That solved the problem of marking in the house, and our superhero dog, "Diaper Boy," was born.

Armed with this knowledge, we attacked the Keegan problem by purchasing two more diapers. We figured one was probably going to constantly be in the wash. That did the trick. Now in the mornings after she slept upstairs, Keegan would have her accident in the diaper on the way down the stairs, and we would finish going potty outside. A quick toss into the wash before heading to work, and by the end of the day, we were back up to full diaper capacity. You would think the system was flawless, but somehow Renea and I still managed to always misplace one, two or sometimes even all three of the diapers. We'd be ready to leave the house, searching around for diapers for Jedi and Keegan. Another fact we had to laugh at was we now had more dogs wearing diapers than not wearing diapers. What had our household turned into? A home full of doggie superheroes, with "Diaper Boy" and "Diaper Girl," that's what. It was a controlled chaos every moment of the day, but we loved the dogs so much, we somehow managed.

Our walks up to the end of the block and back also became a daily occurrence. Now that Keegan was taking steps on her own, I didn't have to support her weight the whole time. With each walk, she seemed to lift her paws higher and higher off the ground until eventually, I was barely holding onto the sling. I was serving more as a guide and brief support towards the end of the walk rather than keeping her off the ground. We were almost there.

I wanted Keegan to get as much exercise as possible. She was taking baby steps but still didn't have the strength in her back legs to officially walk. I began the routine of taking her outside to play fetch with a tennis ball. The only problem with playing fetch with Keegan is that she never fully grasped the concept of the game. You throw the ball, she chases it and then runs off with it. Of course, now that she wasn't on her feet so to speak, I had the advantage. I threw the ball about ten feet, and she would go hopping/crawling/running after it. It was an odd mix of all three, and it thought it was just beautiful. My dog, once paralyzed, now in the backyard with me playing fetch.

Well, Keegan's version of fetch anyway. Once the ball was in her mouth, she tried to run past me back to the house. I think she wanted to run back to her lair in the basement and slobber all over her new prize. I was now faster than she was and jumped in front of her to stop her from running away. I'd wrestle the ball out of her mouth and toss it again. Off she went again in her hybrid scamper, grasping the ball in her jaws and attempting another quick getaway. We went back and forth until she started huffing and puffing, the signal that we were done for the day. Between our long walks and games of fetch, she was getting the much-needed workout.

Little by little, Keegan's legs were getting stronger. She could stand for long periods of time, and her steps were starting to resemble a walk instead of a crawl. Up until now, I'd been using our side yard to let her walk around, express her and let her poop. Our back yard was surrounded by a fence, and this is where we typically let the dogs out. Although we poop-scooped the yard every other day, we didn't want her slipping or falling in dog poop. Now that Keegan was strong enough to navigate around the dangerous doggie land mines in the yard, she was ready for her return to her old stomping grounds.

The first time I opened the gate and let Keegan into the yard, she just milled about the part of the fence closest to the house, sniffing around cautiously. It had been four months since she was in the back by herself, and she wasn't quite sure what to expect. With each trip outside, she would venture out further into the yard, until after a few weeks she seemed back to her old self, barking at birds or leaves blowing by. Once she was comfortable with her new/old surroundings, we decided to reintroduce Canada and Jedi. Jedi was playing nice with Keegan upstairs, but I was still anxious that he would get a little too rough with her outside. I let Jedi and Canada outside first, then cracked the gate and let Keegan join the two. Canada approached Keegan first, and Keegan let out a little growl. I stood by the gate like a nervous father, waiting to jump in at first sight of trouble. Canada wandered away, and now it was Jedi's turn to come up and investigate. Keegan froze as Jedi rushed up to her, and I stood ready to fly in and mediate if things got out of hand. Surprisingly, Jedi sniffed around a bit, then turned away and wandered off to investigate other things in the yard. Keegan relaxed and continued along the fence border, and I breathed a sigh of relief. I kept one eye on the trio the rest of their stay outside, but the reintroduction went well, and yet another piece of normal life returned for Keegan.

Keegan's Journal

March 13, 2008

Dear Diary,

I have been at Animal Fitness Center for 4 days and feel GREAT!! I am on my own in the underwater treadmill with Quintana's supervision. She still looks after me while I am here. I am doing walks in there for 15-17 minutes, but they don't wear me out. I still try to walk back to my kennel when we are through. My water therapy is two times a day and then an Alpha-Stim treatment when I am done. I am getting so strong!

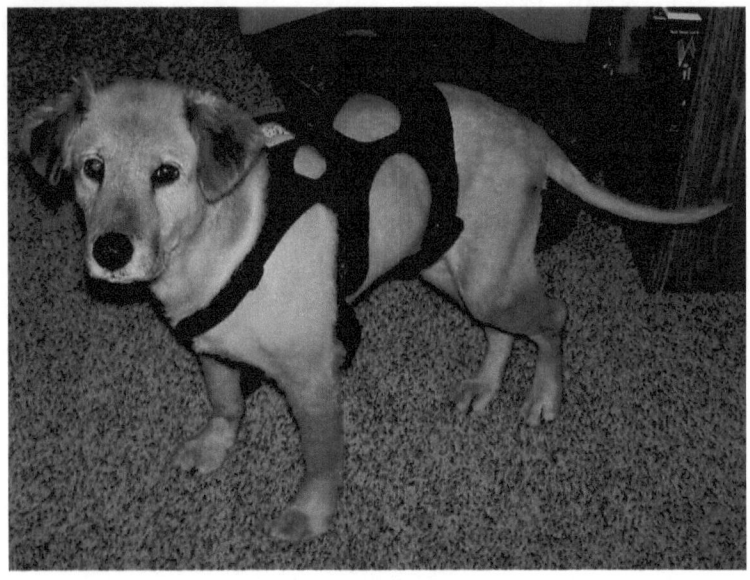

On my feet again!

Chapter 20
This Might Be the Best We Get

It was around this time that we noticed Canada was starting to struggle when getting up from a sitting position. I was paranoid about this scenario repeating itself; if Keegan could suffer such a devastating injury, one of our other pets could too. I thought that Canada might have injured her back somehow. She had always battled a weight problem, and German Shepherds are prone to hip problems. She had seemed lethargic the past few months, but I attributed it to Keegan's injury and being stuck indoors so much during the winter months. We decided a trip to the vet for a checkup would be a good idea.

Thankfully, Canada was injury-free. Unfortunately, we'd been spending so much time with Keegan that Canada had been a bit neglected, including our regular walks. The vet told us Canada was about twenty pounds overweight. We were very relieved to discover that outside of a little extra padding, Canada was completely healthy. However, after reading up on all the causes of paralysis in animals, we knew that Keegan's diagnosis of FCE allowed for a full recovery. Disk injuries were much more severe and had a lesser success rate for recovery. Canada's extra weight made her more likely to suffer a back injury. We discussed a weight loss plan with our vet, and from that point on, we increased her daily exercise and started keeping a closer eye on her weight loss.

Up until Keegan's stroke, Jedi was our most troublesome dog. He was wild, rambunctious, not fully housebroken, moody, and would snap at you when surprised or scared. Now, God bless him, he was the "normal" one. Keegan's rehab continued, Canada now needed extra exercise and was on a weight loss program, and Jedi was just...Jedi. It's funny how our ecosystem had changed in five short months.

Now that Keegan was moving around so well, I decided to start bringing her upstairs during the day. I was a bit nervous because Renea and I were both at work during this time, but I knew she couldn't get past the barrier we created blocking the stairs. The first few days went fine. I would bring Keegs up after taking her outside in the morning, take her out to potty at lunch, and let her spend the afternoon downstairs on her bed. We would bring her back up in the evening, and felt we had a happy balance of Keegan spending time upstairs with the other pets, and downstairs on her orthopedic bed, where she was most comfortable. Midway through the first week, I took Keegan upstairs, grabbed my coffee and headed out the door for work. I got about three blocks from the house, and then it hit me: I forgot to put the barrier up at the top of the stairs. I quickly turned the truck around and sped home. I was only gone five minutes and thought surely Keegan would be safe and sound upstairs. When I made it back home, it was a different story.

I flung the outside basement door open and headed to the door that led to the stairs and foyer. I didn't hear Keegan howling in pain, so I assumed all was well. When I opened the basement door, however, I almost tripped over a 50-pound dog. There she was, sitting at the *bottom* of the stairs.

"Keegan!" I said, shocked. "What are you doing down here?" I took the handle on her vest and helped her to her feet. "Are you ok?"

I walked her back to the basement and to her beds and gave her a thorough once-over to make sure she wasn't hurt. She seemed to survive the excursion unscathed. I joked that nobody told Keegan her back legs didn't fully work, but it was true; she really didn't realize it. I have no idea how she made it down two sets of stairs on two legs, but she did and without a scratch. We certainly had one resourceful dog. With each new accomplishment, she was showing us that her will to improve was unmatched, and there were more surprises to come.

We had worked so hard in her rehab but could only take partial credit. Keegan's will just would not break; even when she had no feeling beyond her upper back, she remained the same sweet dog and took everything in stride. If we were smart, we would pay attention and might just learn a thing or two from our animals.

As spring transitioned to summer, Keegan spent more and more time outside. We had a couple of early setbacks. She fell into a hole that Jedi had dug and couldn't get out. Thankfully Renea was outside working in the yard when it happened and was able to lift her out of the hole quickly. Often Keegan would attempt to squat to pee, but her legs weren't strong enough to hold her up in that position, and she would fall over. Her back legs were getting stronger, but still not strong enough to squat. It was a big step, though. She could only pee when her bladder was full, and nature would take over. We still had to manually express her to empty the bladder fully. But at least she was trying. She would also try to poop, but couldn't hold herself high enough off the ground, so in the end, she would wind up with poop smeared on her hindquarters. She was making a valiant effort to potty on her own, and I didn't mind cleaning her up now and then after a failed attempt.

I told myself if this is the best she gets, I can live with that. We were at a place in her rehab where we could comfortably continue for the rest of Keegan's life if we had to. She was hobbling around, not messing in the house every day, cohabiting with the other animals, and trying her best to be a healthy dog again. My biggest fear had been that she would remain paralyzed entirely and never regain the use of her back legs. Had that happened, things would be a bit different in our household, but we would have made the best of it. My main concern was for Keegan's well-being first, and ours second. I had been seeing a chiropractor on a regular basis for a back problem at the time of Keegan's stroke and for financial reasons decided to forego treatment while we nursed Keegan back to health. Renea and I would sometimes joke that Keegan was getting better health care than us, but that was the mindset we adopted. I didn't care about my back pain. My only focus since January 31 had been to make sure Keegan was as comfortable as possible. If she had remained paralyzed, we would have adjusted our life to accommodate for that. Because of her will, Keegan had regained enough use of her back legs to get around on her own. I was excited about her continued improvement and so very thankful in reflecting on how far she had come in five short months.

Keegan's Journal

April 15, 2008

Dear Diary,

In addition to doing the underwater treadmill at Dr. Ava's, now I'm walking on a real treadmill at home – with some help from my parents of course. Mom holds my harness from above while my Dad guides my back legs. I overheard them saying how proud they are of me for going from range of motion exercise to walking on a treadmill in only three months. I have to be honest, I'm kind of proud of myself too!

Chapter 21
A Walk in the Park

By this point Keegan had become somewhat of a local celebrity at Quincy University. I talked to anyone that would listen over the past five months about her improvement, so I thought it was now time to show her off to everyone. On June 23, I let her out into the backyard and followed her around with a video camera and tennis ball. We played a few rounds of fetch, and I taped her walking around the yard. I think she was showing off a bit for the camera; her legs only gave out on her once in chasing down the ball, but she jumped right back up and continued before stopping in front of the camera and dropping the ball. The same dog, mind you, that typically runs the other way once she captures her prize. Quite the showoff, indeed.

Once I had enough footage, I headed inside to put together a video update of Keegan to share with everyone. I included a brief title page with the date of her injury, prognosis, and update on her rehab. I added a few photos before the video to show a glimpse of the "before," with Renea hand-feeding Keegan in the beginning, her first trip to Dr. Ava's in the hydrotherapy treadmill, sitting in her wheelchair, and trying to crawl across the living room floor. Each photo had text assigned to it describing what was happening. Finally, and extremely proud, I added the date of the video, and footage of

Keegan chasing the tennis ball in the backyard. I posted it on YouTube and sent a link to Renea. The next day we both e-mailed the video to family, friends, co-workers; basically all the people we made listen to us ramble on for months about Keegan.

The response was tremendous. Many people called or e-mailed us to let us know the video made them cry or that they were sharing it with all the animal lovers they knew. The fact that Keegan, who was doing such an amazing job inspiring us, was now inspiring other people put a smile on my face. She deserved the attention! We were also surprised to see so many other dogs were on YouTube. There were dogs at various stages of recovery, instructional videos on how to strap a down dog into a wheelchair, dogs with broken backs that had mastered the spinal walk; it was incredible. While it was sad to see such a large collection of injured pets, it was wonderful to see so many owners who loved their animals enough to show them off in this fashion. We had no idea dogs could even suffer injuries such as this before Keegan had her stroke. This was just another way to educate people about these types of animal injuries.

Renea and I talked about the desire to raise more awareness about this cause and hoped we were doing just that, albeit on a small level. Keegan's injury set us back thousands of dollars, and at the time of her injury, we were a dual income-no child family. I don't know what a couple with children would have done in our situation. Unfortunately, it's hard enough to raise everyday awareness about the need for animal adoption at your local shelter, much less a cause as targeted as something like paralysis in household pets. Still, something could be done to help make people aware of the problem and ease the burden on families fighting so hard to give their pets a comfortable life after a devastating injury.

We decided a checkup with Dr. Ava would be a good move at this point. Keegan was moving around so much…*walking* around so much…we wanted to be sure she wasn't in danger of damaging any tendons or ligaments in her back legs. We also knew she was ready for the next step in rehab. Renea drove down in late June for the checkup. Dr. Ava did some chiropractic adjustments on Keegan and gave Renea some new rehab instructions: obstacle course!

Keegan now needed to be challenged with hills and curves to work all the different muscles in her legs and back. This rehab sounded a thousand times more enjoyable than the arduous rehab we'd begun back in February. Finding challenging hills and winding roads to walk Keegan on was a task we were happy to accept.

This visit to Dr. Ava was also the first time "full recovery" was mentioned since she began her rehab. Throughout the entire process, I treated the term full recovery like a bad word. I didn't want to jinx anything, so I just ignored the statement and hoped Keegan would continue getting better.

"If you follow the rehab," Dr. Ava told Renea, "I think Keegan could be fully recovered in three months."

Renea and I spent the next few weeks stopping and admiring Keegan any time she walked around or simply stood outside doing nothing but wagging her tail.

"Can you believe we're at this point?" Renea asked me once while we stood at an upstairs window watching Keegan in the backyard.

"I never thought we'd get here," I answered.

The first couple months served as a real gut check for me. It is human nature to question how you might react to certain situations when they arise; will you remain calm under pressure? Will you make the right decisions with emotions running unchecked? I look back with pride at how I handled Keegan's initial injury and subsequent rehab. I couldn't have done it on my own. Renea was right there with me every morning, shuffling down the stairs still half-asleep to do Keegan's first of three hours of daily rehab. I was fortunate to find the members of the handicapped pets website when I did. Without their tips, stories, and words of encouragement, finding hope would have been much harder. Through it all, Keegan stayed positive, loving and loyal, carving out an indelible mark in our hearts that will never be shared by another animal the same way. We were now getting closer and closer to finishing what we started, which was giving Keegan a normal life.

After returning from their latest trip to see Dr. Ava, Renea went to work right away with Keegan, finding the steepest hills in our neighborhood. Keegs was now walking without the aid of her sling. We would bring her legs along just in case she tired out during the walk, but she was doing a fantastic job on her own. One problem we ran into, however, was her back paws getting sore. She was moving her legs, but she didn't always lift them entirely off the ground, so her back paws would scrape against the concrete. I got back from a long walk with her and noticed one of her nails was bleeding. Later, she developed a second cut on her other paw. We tried using booties, but she quickly rejected them, locking up and telling us, "no way I'm using those things on my feet!"

It was time to call an audible. We would need to walk Keegan on grass instead of concrete until her steps became more prominent. Thankfully we had the big side yard that had a bit of an incline, so there was a small hill there to work with. Walks all around the house now complemented her outside time as well. In addition, we started piling her in the car and taking her to Quincy's South Park, a beautiful park known for its sweeping, hilly terrain. To our surprise, Keegan made it up the hills with more ease than going down. Her back still wasn't strong enough to keep completely straight, so while going down the steep parts of the hills she would do more of a sideways shuffle until we could straighten her out.

Keegan soon began picking up on what it meant when we grabbed a few plastic shopping bags to stuff in our pockets. It was walk time! She would shift around until she could get up off her bed, then saunter on over to the door and wait anxiously to go outside. Trips to South Park became very frequent as the next phase of her rehab. With each session, she seemed to do a bit better navigating the rugged terrain. Her back became steadier going downhill, leading to less of the "sideway shuffle." These trips to the park were rehab for both Keegan and myself. She was getting the physical workout she needed and rebuilding muscle mass. It was serving as an emotional rehab of sorts for me. I never knew that something as simple as taking your dog to the park for a walk could be such a cathartic experience. During the walks, I would reflect on all the events that led up to that point. I thought back to the early mornings and late evenings, the financial struggles, the three hours a day of rehab. I wanted Keegan to walk again more than anything in the world, and now because we made it through all the seemingly impossible obstacles, here we were, walking in the park.

Getting stronger with each walk in the park

Keegan's Journal

May 23, 2008

Dear Diary,

    I no longer need the Bottoms-Up Leash to help me get around outside. I walk kind of awkward but I have mastered it, my left leg is not as good as the right one but I am still trying. I would really like to chase the squirrels and rabbits. I still don't have control over my bowels or bladder so Mom and Dad are helping me out. They are the BEST!!! My legs aren't strong enough to support myself when I bend down to go potty but I will get stronger! I miss Dr. Ava and Quintana so I have Dad e-mail them with all of my good news. I know they are happy for me too.

Chapter 22
You Take the Good, You Take the Bad

Keegan had reached a point where she would have good days and bad days. I could often tell what to expect for the day just by watching her navigate through the backyard during her morning bathroom break. Her left rear leg was weaker than the other, and on the bad days, the leg drifted underneath her body in a crisscross fashion, tripping her up as she walked. She also struggled with her balance on those days, leading to a wobbly rear end, especially when pivoting to change direction. Thankfully there were more good days than bad, but I held my breath on those rough days, worried she might be regressing. Even though she had made tremendous progress, this was still my biggest fear.

Another way to tell if Keegs was having a good day was where I found her downstairs. She was now feeling good enough to roam around the basement, so whenever I walked downstairs and didn't see her lying on her one of her beds, I knew she was up and wandering around, and that was a good sign.

I started to get glimpses of the old Keegan during some of these good days. While her mood remained positive throughout the entire process, she still wasn't exactly her normal self. The old Keegan had a zest for life. When you walked into a room, her face would light up, and she would start bouncing around in excitement. There was a look in her eyes that told you, "I'm so excited you're here!" Understandably, that enthusiasm disappeared with her injury. She was still a sweet girl, and her spirits were high, but that zest for life was gone. Now, it was coming back, one good day at a time. Sometimes it would last for hours, sometimes only for a moment when playing tug-of-war, but the fact that it was returning spoke volumes about where she was mentally.

I first noticed this on a Saturday afternoon in July. I was sitting at the downstairs computer when Keegan got up off her bed and wandered over to the glass basement door. This was not out of the ordinary, as she often barked at things she saw outside the door. Instead of barking, though, she snorted. Then she hurried (as quick as she could at this point in her rehab) to the other side of the room and snorted again. Now she had my attention, so I wheeled my chair around to see what all the fuss was about. When she returned to her bed and plopped back down, I noticed that familiar mischievous look in her eyes that had been missing since January. I still didn't know what she was up to when all the sudden she got up again and hurried past me to the other side of the room. Now I saw the culprit; she was chasing a fly around the basement! She carried on like this for nearly a half-hour before finally giving up and retiring to the bed for good, but it signified another huge moment in her rehabilitation. The playful side of her personality was slowly coming back. My dog was chasing a fly around the basement, and I couldn't have been more excited. Renea was out of town at the time, and when she called later that day, I shared the exciting news.

"Your dog was chasing a fly around the basement!" I told her.

"Awww," she responded.

Two grown adults, sharing a conversation about their dog chasing a fly around the room. Thankfully Big Brother wasn't eavesdropping on our conversation, or we might have been flagged for potential insanity. I could see us trying to plead our case in court...*But you don't understand, your Honor, she was chasing a FLY!*

I went for a jog on a gorgeous July evening that offered a warm purple glow as the sun set in the west. When I returned to the basement, I noticed Keegan was shifting around her bed, restless. I grabbed her leash and figured a walk around the premises would help. When we got outside, I noticed the pace of her walk was picking up. She was no longer walking, but actually trotting through the grass! I looked around to see if anyone in our neighborhood was watching. I wanted to yell, "She's trotting!" at the top of my lungs but didn't want the mental health unit from the local hospital called. Instead, I picked up the pace of my walk to keep up with her. Occasionally her bad leg would trip her up, but she quickly recovered and continued. I suddenly felt like I had a show dog next to me as part of some grand display. I jogged slowly alongside Keegan as if showing her off to a panel of judges. She was showing off, so why couldn't I pretend as well? We sauntered around the house a couple of times until she started panting. I knelt beside her and gave praise for such a good job, and she trotted back inside to her lair, with a tail wag and no doubt a strong sense of accomplishment. That familiar look of a happy dog was back in her eyes that evening.

Keegan's Journal

June 24, 2008

Dear Diary,

I'm walking again! Dr. Frick says the next phase of my rehab is obstacle courses with lots of hills and turns, so my parents have been taking me to the park on daily walks! I'm starting to squat and pee when my bladder is full too. Little by little, it's all coming back to me. I can't tell you how excited I am to be going on walks with my sister again! I still have a little trouble like when I fell in a hole dug by my brother. I think he did it on purpose to antagonize me. I pee whenever I get excited, like when people come to the house to see how good I'm doing...but my parents are so excited about me walking again that I don't think they mind cleaning up the occasional mess.

Chapter 23
The Pet Parade

In the fall of 2008, eight months after Keegan's stroke, a student from my public relations class came to me to help publicize an event. He was planning a community dog walk to help raise money for the local animal shelter. The event was dubbed the Padua Pet Parade as it would begin at Quincy University's Padua Hall dormitory and circle the entire campus. We worked together to publicize the event months in advance with the plan of raising big money for our woefully underfunded shelter. It was while working on the publicity for the event that I got the wildest of ideas: Keegan participating in the parade.

It was a longshot. We were only eight months out from her stroke and just a few months in to her walking on her own again. I had no idea if she would be ready physically or mentally. How would she hold up on a near mile-long walk? Would she be able to handle the stress and co-exist with the other dogs? I was determined to give it a try and I knew Keegan was too. As my student worked diligently that fall in preparation for a massive fundraiser, Keegan and I trained for a dog walk. It might sound silly, but for Keegan it was like climbing Mt. Everest. I continued our walks through rough terrain in the parks. I stretched out our neighborhood walks in small increments to build up her stamina. It was the final push we needed to complete Keegan's rehab. As was the story with her entire journey, little by little Keegan showed improvements. Our walks lasted longer each time. I don't think she was physically navigating the rough terrain better but rather learning how to control her own body with this new style of wobble-walking she was perfecting. She fell less often as we encountered obstacles and carried herself with greater balance.

I was watching the new version of the dog we'd have for the rest of her life take shape. Keegan would labor a bit to get off the ground, but once she was up she was off and running. Her left rear leg seemed to take the brunt of the damage from the stroke. It never did return to a normal step but rather an awkward jab down towards the ground, as if perennially trying to find solid footing. Her rear right leg did most of the heavy lifting for her hindquarters, but it was enough for her to get around with a proud trot. If she tried to take off running suddenly, the brain signals couldn't get to her back legs in time and the legs would simply give out and drag behind as she pulled herself towards whatever had her attention. She could stand firm for a fair amount of time, but any kind of contact would send her wobbling to one side, forcing her to shuffle her legs around and re-establish her footing. But most important, she remained the same sweet dog and was rediscovering her zest for life. She did not snap at other dogs if they accidentally knocked her over. Her new unique navigation skills were really quite funny. Keegan was always easily distracted but now she'd train her attention on one thing, get disturbed or knocked over by another dog, and by the time she recovered her balance, she'd found something else to turn her attention to. Scatterbrain, meet scatterbody.

She still loved walks, hanging out with the other dogs, and snuggling with us and our other animals. Though her physical capabilities may have changed over the past year, her playful nature and loving soul came out the other side unscathed. I thought there was no better way to celebrate that than a pleasant walk with Keegan and dozens of other dogs.

And so, on a blustery Saturday mid-November morning, I loaded Keegan into the back of the SUV yet again, only this time for a celebration. We arrived at Quincy University and I beamed as we joined the other dogs and their owners at Padua Hall. Many there knew Keegan's story and stopped to chat and give Keegan some love. One of QU's friars and a close friend and a confidant during Keegan's ordeal, Brother Ed, gave a blessing of the animals before the walk. I already knew how blessed we truly were just to be there, ready to accomplish what was unthinkable just months earlier. Tears welled up in my eyes as we shuffled into pairs to begin the pet parade. And then it began. We walked. Keegan walked.

Keegan in the Padua Pet Parade, Nov. 15, 2008

It may not have been your typical dog walk, but these days nothing about Keegan was typical. It didn't matter. We may have had to stop a few times when an uncontrollable bowel movement occurred. And we may have had to take a short cut through the middle of campus because the full mile was just too taxing on her. But by God we made it, Keegan walked in a pet parade, eight months after we were told by a doctor to end her life because there would be no quality to it. After months of therapy with complete strangers. Hours and hours spent in an underwater treadmill and repetitive exercises. Countless trips in the back of our SUV to and from doctors. All for today. All for a walk with me. How blessed we were.

Chapter 24
Some Tips

When our journey with Keegan's stroke started I wish we had some guidance. We were fortunate enough to stumble across some resources along the way and eventually found Dr. Ava, but it felt like we were flying blind in the beginning. The first week after Keegan returned home from the hospital was by far the toughest. To survive, we had to establish a routine. Everything revolved around that routine, and it allowed us to give Keegan the best care possible while maintaining our sanity. As each week passed, we seemed to develop more and more systematic ways to manage the seemingly insurmountable task of caring for our down dog. In the following chapter, I will discuss some of the existing strategies we found as well as ideas we discovered on our own to make Keegan's care pleasant for her and manageable for us. It is by no means an instruction manual on how to care for a down dog. If you ever find yourself in our situation, I hope you can take a few of the things we tried and work them into your routine.

The decision to place Keegan in a centralized location with easy access to the back door was huge for us. Dogs like the familiar; it gives them a sense of calm. Giving Keegan her own dedicated space seemed to give her peace at a time when her entire world was turned upside down. For us, it made getting her outside as efficient as possible. This was especially key when she was in the act of peeing or pooping. Another factor that weighed in the decision was that our computer desk and a television were downstairs. We wanted Keegan to be in a place where we could spend a lot of time in the same room with her. I knew we couldn't spend every waking moment with her, but I didn't want her to be alone too much during such a scary and confusing time. Renea and I went back and forth for a while about where she should go. In the beginning, Renea argued for putting her beds in the downstairs bathroom. My reply was that she might as well be in jail, stuck in a tiny room surrounded by four walls day and night. I knew Keegan's rehab would be long, if not something she might do for the rest of her life. I wanted her front in center, regardless of the messes we'd have to clean up or the fact that we'd be giving up the practical use of our basement for an undetermined amount of time. Many factors weigh into the decision of where to make a home base for your down dog, and every situation is different, but try to keep the dog's feelings in mind when choosing the location that will serve as "home" for the next few months or longer.

To create Keegan's lair, we enclosed two giant sized orthopedic beds with plastic milk crates and large rubber tubs typically reserved for storage. Renea came up with the great idea to spread plastic shower curtains underneath the beds. You can easily find these cheap at any local dollar store. We purchased several of them and lined not only underneath the beds, but also the on top of the carpet between the beds and the back door and her exercise area. I can't count the number of accidents Keegan had on the exercise ball or on her way outside, and thankfully it was on the plastic shower curtains. It is easy to clean up, and you save your carpet from countless stains.

We purchased higher quality shower curtains to wrap the beds in. Covering the beds is imperative; it is where the majority of a down dog's accidents will occur in the beginning. We flipped the beds over on top of the plastic, folded the plastic under and used duct tape to hold it in position. Next, we tossed blankets on top of the area, so Keegan still had a warm, cozy place to lie.

We turned a basement bar countertop near Keegan's area into a utility station. It is very handy to have all your supplies in one location. Your dog's life isn't the only one turned upside down during this time. Your mind will be spinning for quite a while, so knowing exactly where to go anytime a situation arises is very helpful. Whether it's cleaning supplies, treats or the spare diapers, we always knew where to run to first.

As Keegan improved, we increased the circumference of the area to include a portion of the regular flooring. When her ability to stand and later walk returned, it was difficult for her to walk across the cushioned surface of her beds. We still had the shower curtain linings covering the carpet, so accidents were easily cleaned up. Because she liked to stand when eating and drinking, we pulled the bedding away from her dishes, giving her more practice standing and balancing on a hard surface.

Large quantities of paper towels and rags also come in handy. Again, these can all be purchased at a dollar store or in bulk at one of the wholesale warehouses. Whether you're cleaning up pee or wiping your dog's fur coat, you'll need both paper and cloth towels early and often.

A laundry tub dedicated to dirty diapers, bedding and towels was tucked away in a designated area. When you're running around with a pee-soaked blanket, the last thing you want to do is carry it through the house to the bathroom hamper. In the first couple months, the tub would be at least half full each night, so we made a habit of tossing the contents of the tub in the washer before bed and throwing the load in the dryer before work the next day. It was a great system that kept the tub empty and Keegan's bedding and diapers clean.

A quick survey of our supply table would look something like this: paper towels, cloth towels (both small and large), waterless shampoo, surface cleaning solution, carpet cleaning solution, Lysol disinfectant spray, disposable dog diapers (later replaced with cloth diapers), blankets, dog treats (mostly chewable bones and rawhide to help her pass the time), KONG toy, jar of creamy peanut butter (can be used in KONG and to cover pills with), assorted vitamins and supplements, and the Alpha-Stim unit.

As far as a down dog's rehabilitation should go, I've made it clear how I don't feel the original advice given to us by Dr. Holt's office was suffice for Keegan's rehab. While I am no doctor and therefore cannot prescribe what should or should not be done for your pet, I can say with good faith that you should do as much investigating as possible regarding the proper treatment for your dog's injury. Had I listened to our original therapist's advice, I'm certain that Keegan would not have walked again. Range of motion exercises just won't cut it for a down dog with the potential to walk again. I searched online for every resource I could find to discover what kind of help was available for our dog; I suggest you do the same. Don't take what you are told at face value. Do the research and find out what type of rehabilitation is right for your dog and your family. Disc injuries are completely different from FCE's and require extensive crate rest.

I also recommend the website handicappedpets.com as a great starting point. The best thing Keegan's neurologist did for us was to make us aware of the handicappedpets.com resource. While I found Dr. Ava Frick by doing my own research, handicappedpets.com introduced me to a wealth of information and more importantly, a support group that quite honestly helped us survive the entire rehabilitation process. Without the connection to other pet owners suffering through the same ordeal, I don't know where we would be today. The website is now a site for animal wheelchairs but there is still a valuable discussion forum with amazing people you can turn to for advice. The original members of the website gave our family hope and faith, and they are among the small group of key people we owe thanks to for Keegan's success. It is quite a collection of wonderful people that make sacrifices every day so that their handicapped pets live a happy and full life. I am humbled by them and cannot thank them enough for their support. I have no doubt that whatever your situation you will be in good hands with the pet owners on this website.

Over the eight months of Keegan's rehabilitation, I underwent a bit of rehab myself. I developed a patience level that I had lacked my entire life. It changed my entire outlook on the very fast-paced world we currently live in. Keegan's paralysis forced me to slow down and look at things from a different perspective. My bad days instantly turned into great days whenever Keegan would make some small accomplishment.

Keegan's injury tested my marriage, and in the end, I like to think it made it stronger. Renea and I always said it was us against the world, but that truly wasn't the case up until now. We'd never been forced to come together as a team to accomplish something of this magnitude. While we didn't always agree with each other, we always agreed on the end result, and we learned to put Keegan's health ahead of everything: our time, our finances, our other animals, and each other. We both put our heads down and took a leap of faith that we hoped would end with a healthy dog. Was there any other way?

For the rest of my life, I will never take another walk with a dog for granted. Taking a dog for a walk now has a different meaning. Maybe it's just me, or maybe I now fully understand why dogs enjoy their walks so much. Either way, I enjoy being just as excited as the dog just before walking out the door.

I shared a special bond with my dog Bud. He was with me for 17 years and saw me through my awkward high school years. I'm convinced Cha will forever be the most amazing creature I'll ever know. I feel that although he was deaf, I communicated more with him than any animal I've ever had. Jedi's story still brings tears to my eyes. The fact that he knew to come back to our house a second time looking for shelter, safety and love says so much about an animal's keen instinct. To find out that he was knocking on death's door with stage two heartworms just makes it even more incredible. So many animals have touched my life and helped make our house a home. I will never know a stronger bond, however, than the one I share with Keegan.

Keegan's injury was devastating in so many ways. It took away her ability to walk. It pushed us to the brink financially. It changed the entire ecosystem we worked so hard to build with our animals. It also taught me what I was made of. I don't question how I'll respond in the clutch anymore. It taught me to never count an animal out, despite what others tell you. In many ways, it restored my faith in people. So many people rallied around us when we were fighting to nurture Keegan back to health. In the end, I'm just amazed at how much was truly gained from one dog, her injury, and the will to triumph over insurmountable odds to live a normal, happy life. After all, even though *we* knew, nobody ever told Keegan that her legs didn't work.

Chapter 25
The Rest of Our Lives

It took a lot longer than I ever planned to write this book. I began shortly after Keegan's recovery was "complete." But after putting our lives on hold for nearly a year, things sped up pretty fast, almost as if to catch up. I completed my master's degree and began a new path as a full-time professor in Quincy University's Communication Department. Renea was promoted to an administrator position at her school. I got a second master's degree and was promoted and awarded tenure. And the biggest change for us came in 2011 when we had our first child, Lucas.

Maybe it's just age, maybe it had something to do with our experience with Keegan, but eventually Renea and I concluded that we were ready to advance from the animal world and try our hand at raising a human. So, the ecosystem changed yet again with the addition of a little person to our household. And everyone continued to co-exist just fine. Lucas found a new pillow in Canada, our cats found a new pillow in Lucas, and as our family expanded so did the love.

Unfortunately, despite our best efforts you just cannot slow Father Time. Our moments with the animals in our lives must seem so precious because we get such sparing time with them. They just don't live as long as us and we eventually must confront the pain of losing them. For a family like ours, full of animals, each with a unique story, the pain would be great over the next several years. One by one, age caught up with all of them. Jedi aged quickly near the end, I assume because of the abuse and toll the heartworms took on his body when he was younger. Canada's age and hips eventually robbed her of any quality of life, as it often does in German Shepherds. Akili and Cali simply passed on as they aged, having lived long, incredibly comfy lives as housecats.

We gave Keegan another six good years of life before the combination of age and the damage from the stroke began to take the joy from her life. In 2014 we finally were forced to make the impossible decision to spare her any more pain and have her put to sleep. I'd never dreaded anything more in my life. I knew it was for the best, that it was unfair to keep her around simply for our benefit. She was ready, her struggle needed to come to an end. With the heaviest of hearts, I carried Keegan into our veterinarian one last time and laid with her on the floor before the veterinarian came in and allowed her to drift off to sleep for good. I thanked her for all the lessons she'd taught us through the years…for her love and patience…for her unwavering loyalty. As I laid with her I reflected on her unbreakable spirit during her rehab process. She made it possible for us to do what we needed to do. It was all three of us, working in tandem, for one common goal. Maybe she knew her legs didn't work after all, she was just as determined as we were to get them moving again.

As I write this, P.J. is lying next to me purring away, still going strong at 16 years old, the last animal standing. We always joked that she was forever a kitten, but now I think she believes it. You'd never know she was a geriatric cat. She still runs around the house, gets into general mischief, and loves to play. But we know. You can't stop

Father Time, and it's only a matter of time before he catches up to her as well. When that day comes, we'll have her cremated and buried with the others on my family's land, all of them finally together again. We'll likely take a few months to allow us all to mourn and see what it's like to be animal free for the first time in our lives. And then, we'll set about round two of taking in a new group of rescues. They've got a tall order though, our previous group set the bar impossibly high. Especially Keegan, which was impressive considering her legs didn't work. Just do me a favor, don't tell her that.

Our son Lucas and Keegan, October 2012

About the Author

Travis C. Yates is an Associate Professor of Communication at Quincy University. Prior to teaching he spent ten years in the television news industry as a producer, reporter and videographer. He is an Emmy-winning writer and moonlights as a multimedia artist, producing screenplays, commercials, and short films.

He is also the author of *A Latchkey Kid's Take on Modern Cinema*, a collection of essays and reviews that examines the works of more than 120 directors of contemporary and classic films.

www.ingramcontent.com/pod-product-compliance
Lightning Source LLC
Chambersburg PA
CBHW030324080526
44584CB00012B/706